Cambridge Elements

Elements in Critica
edite
Kristian Kristiansen, *Ur*
Michael Ro\
Francis Nyamnjoh, *Un..........., ...*
Astrid Swenson, *Bath University*
Shu-Li Wang, *Academia Sinica*
Ola Wetterberg, *University of Gothenburg*

ETHNOGRAPHIC RETURNS

Memory Processes and Archive Film

Anne Gustavsson

National University of General San Martín/National Scientific and Technological Research Council, Argentina

CAMBRIDGE
UNIVERSITY PRESS

CAMBRIDGE
UNIVERSITY PRESS

University Printing House, Cambridge CB2 8BS, United Kingdom

One Liberty Plaza, 20th Floor, New York, NY 10006, USA

477 Williamstown Road, Port Melbourne, VIC 3207, Australia

314–321, 3rd Floor, Plot 3, Splendor Forum, Jasola District Centre, New Delhi – 110025, India

103 Penang Road, #05–06/07, Visioncrest Commercial, Singapore 238467

Cambridge University Press is part of the University of Cambridge.

It furthers the University's mission by disseminating knowledge in the pursuit of education, learning, and research at the highest international levels of excellence.

www.cambridge.org
Information on this title: www.cambridge.org/9781108823425
DOI: 10.1017/9781108914086

First published 2021

A catalogue record for this publication is available from the British Library.

ISBN 978-1-108-82342-5 Paperback
ISSN 2632-7074 (online)
ISSN 2632-7066 (print)

Ethnographic Returns

Memory Processes and Archive Film

Elements in Critical Heritage Studies

DOI: 10.1017/9781108914086
First published online: August 2021

Anne Gustavsson
*National University of General San Martín/National Scientific and
Technological Research Council, Argentina*

Author for correspondence: Anne Gustavsson, anne.gustavsson@gmail.com

Abstract: In the past decades, cultural heritage stored at museums and archives has been returned to source communities in various forms and under diverse circumstances. This contribution to the Elements series explores and discusses specifically the return of digital "ethnographic" images to Indigenous and non-Indigenous people that share a common recent history of coexistence and dispute over the same territory. The author argues that the affective reception of what a given archive labels as tangible and intangible heritage varies according to each audience's particular memory practices, historical experience and way of relating to shared hegemonic notions of "whiteness" and "indigeneity."

Keywords: affectivity, archive film, ethnography, heritage, memory

ISBNs: 9781108823425 (PB), 9781108914086 (OC)
ISSNs: 2632-7074 (online), 2632-7066 (print)

Contents

1 Introduction: "Revisiting Ethnographic Sites, Decentering Authorized Interpretations?"

1.1 A Film on the Road

The topics I explore in this Element were ignited by an encounter that took place in 2007. I was on a work placement at the Juan B. Ambrosetti Museum of Ethnography in Buenos Aires (Argentina), when two Swedish documentary filmmakers showed up asking for expert knowledge on the Gran Chaco[1] region and its Indigenous population. They were on their way to Formosa, a province located in the Argentine section of the Gran Chaco,[2] looking for the Indigenous communities where a Swedish expedition had shot a film ninety years earlier. Since we shared the same nationality and spoke the same language, I was called upon to assist them. They showed me fragments of the old black and white archive film, explaining to me that the images portrayed the Pilagá.[3] They had obtained a copy of the film from the archive of the Museum of World Culture (MWC) in Gothenburg, Sweden. The aim of their trip to Formosa was to prepare the grounds for a possible documentary film in which images filmed in 1920 would be contrasted with those depicting present-day communities in the same region. At a later point I found out that they had indeed been able to visit various Pilagá communities in Formosa. Nonetheless, their initial intention of selling the project to the Swedish Television hadn't proved successful.

This personal encounter not only made me curious about learning more about the film's full content and the expedition during which it was shot but also made me reflect upon the way ethnographic archive materials had come to circulate visually and digitally outside the institutions that had historically cared for their conservation, labeling and interpretation. As the years went by and I initiated archival research on the expedition, obtained my own copy of the film and eventually took it with me during my fieldwork in Formosa many more questions arose that guided the research process as it unfolded between 2013 and 2018, resulting in my PhD in Social Anthropology at the Institute for High Social Studies at the National University of General San Martín, Argentina (Gustavsson, 2018a). In this Element I explore some of these questions, such as: What happens when ethnographic sites are revisited? How can ethnographic data and methods be updated and reframed? How can contemporary social

---

[1] The Gran Chaco is a lowland alluvial plain region that comprises parts of Argentina, Paraguay, Bolivia and Brazil.

[2] The Argentine Chaco includes the provinces of Formosa and Chaco, the east of Salta and Santiago del Estero, and the northern portion of the province of Santa Fe.

[3] The Pilagá live in central Formosa and are currently one of four officially recognized Indigenous peoples in this province. According to traditional ethnolinguistic categories, the Pilagá belong to the guaycurú linguistic group.

practices and memory-making confront and contest institutional definitions of intangible and tangible cultural heritage? These questions have also taken shape in dialogue with the current debate and literature on "digital repatriation" projects, Indigenous claims to access and management of their cultural heritage, and the use of visual archive sources in social and ethnographic research.

1.2 Ethnographic Returns: Phenomenon and Research Approaches

Alongside the rise and diversified uses of new technologies, over the last few decades the return of digitalized museum objects and visual collections to communities that have historically been ethnographized has become a growing phenomenon in certain regions of the world. It engages a range of actors and has turned into a topic of recent scholarship (e.g., Christen, 2011, Edwards, 2003, Giordano, 2010, Hennessy, 2016, Sbriccoli, 2016, Troya, 2012).

This phenomenon implies a growing flow of digitalized archive and museum materials transiting outside their traditional storage institutions, reverting in some way the unidirectional and colonial circuits by which emblematic images and objects of alterity were historically extracted from ethnographic sites and taken to European or North American museums and other academic institutions (Fernández Bravo, 2013). Materiality as well as intangible expressions of culture were captured and collected in diverse colonial and postcolonial situations between the end of the nineteenth century and the middle of the twentieth century, coinciding with the development of anthropology as a discipline. These have become relevant in new ways at the end of the twentieth century and beginning of the twenty-first in the context of continuous Indigenous struggles for the recognition of their rights and of the global phenomenon of revitalization of Indigenous identities (Prins, 2004).

Currently, there exists a common concern and commitment to the ongoing work of decolonization of museums and academia (Smith, 1999): On one hand, looking for ways to share curatorial and ethnographic authority at museums and, on the other, to reframe forms of collaboration between scholars and Indigenous peoples during fieldwork. Both represent critical approaches to the history of anthropology and to the discipline's central role in the accumulation of cultural heritage in scientific institutions, seeking to break away from the colonialistic paradigm under which many museum collections were formed. Within these shared parameters, I have identified two main trends in research approaches when it comes to ethnographic digital returns: The first one being carried out in museum or archive management contexts by museum professionals, archivists or scholars (Christen, 2011, Edwards, 2003, Hennessy, 2016,

O'Neal, 2013) and, the second, involving ethnographers and anthropologists who share and discuss digitalized archive and museum material or their personal archives during fieldwork (Buckley, 2014, Sbriccoli, 2016). In some cases these approaches overlap (Bell, 2003, Gustafson Reinius, 2015).

In the first case, a large part of the literature is focused on describing and evaluating the outcome of so-called collaborative projects that follow institutional guidelines and policies that are striving to establish dialogues between ethnographic and anthropological museum collections and the people and communities represented in them, often referred to as "source communities" or "descendent communities" (Edwards, 2003). Since these dialogues are to take place without actually carrying out physical repatriation,[4] instead assuring remote visual access to collections through websites, digital archives and online databases, not only has digitalization of museum collections become central but new technologies have also been given greater status, seen as regulators or tools in the construction of less asymmetrical relations. Part of this literature (Christen, 2011, Hennessy, 2016) discusses the collaborative development of technological tools for organizing, interpreting and accessing collections, taking into account Indigenous knowledge systems and striving to respect source communities' ethical considerations on how and by whom digitalized, sensitive cultural heritage is to be accessed online. These scholars stress that access and control are not given by technology itself but rather by the way people use technology, something that is regulated by social relations and cultural norms.

This research approach also tends to be highly institutional and project oriented, often downplaying the larger context in which claims of collaboration or restitution are framed as well as the social impact of returns. Considering that these collaborative projects proliferate globally at the same time as Indigenous people and other "source communities" play active roles in asserting rights over their cultural heritage, it is surprising how seldom political factors and social conflicts are analyzed by scholars involved in the projects. The collaborative projects and the negotiations that they have implied are at times presented from a project management perspective, including suggestions on how to make future collaborations successful and stressing how the institution holding the heritage benefits in terms of complementary and corrected information about collections (O'Neal, 2013). Digital returns have even been referred to as a low-cost and more practical alternative than physical repatriation (Christen, 2011). The fact that many of these scholars are simultaneously entangled in museum practice

---

[4] Although physical repatriation or restitution of especially human remains has been greatly debated in Argentina (e.g., Arenas, 2011, Lazzari, 2008), reflections on digital forms of restitution are less common.

and form part of the projects and institutions that they are writing about might explain why their focus has been more on project progression and outcome and its effects on the museum world than on how new access to digital collections have impacted collective memory practices and the internal sociopolitical dynamics of the actors involved.

Concerning the second research approach, which is field based, anthropologists and other scholars are not only returning materials that were collected by former generations of field-workers but also digitalizing their own ethnographic archives to share them with source communities (Gustafson Reinius, 2015). In this type of return, which might be the result of a claim or not, the emphasis is on the presentation and discussion of digitalized materials produced by anthropological research in nonvirtual environments. This sharing of data is in some cases linked to epistemological reformulations (Sbriccoli, 2016) and is made possible by the fact that different generations of anthropologists often return to the same places to carry out fieldwork.

When it comes to visual collections, including archive film and photography, research undertaken from this second approach has paid attention to the contemporary interpretations of this material when being returned to the field, considering especially the social and political uses of the images in relation to the receptors' identity processes. Here the focus of the research has been on how the reception of the digitalized archive material is conditioned by the existing social tissue and hierarchies as well as the local production of meaning (Buckley, 2014, Sbriccoli, 2016) or how contemporary Indigenous leaders have used the visual legacy produced by "salvage ethnography" to revitalize their own memory and a modern identity of autochthony as well as to claim for the reparation of injustices (Prins, 2004). In other cases, research has highlighted the way photographs pertaining to Western archives have been inserted and appropriated by Indigenous histories (Wright, 2009) and incorporated into processes in which traditional culture is revalorized (Troya, 2012).

With regards to naming these digital practices and projects involving anthropologists, historically ethnographized communities and museums or archives, the use of the term "repatriation" is controversial. Although many scholars (Bell et al., 2013, Christen, 2011, Hennessy, 2016) use the term "digital repatriation" or "virtual repatriation," understood as making digitalized collections available to be accessed visually and virtually by the contemporary communities from which the materials originate, Boast and Enote (2013) warn that using the term "repatriation" to refer to the digital sharing of data and collections can lead to misunderstandings of the meaning of the act of "repatriation" in the sense of a transfer of physical custody. In contrast to physical repatriation, the digital share doesn't imply a change or transfer in ownership, the original material that is made available and accessed through digital representations always stays with the collecting institution. In this sense, the use of the term "repatriation" or "restitution" to designate sharing of surrogates or copies can be misleading.

On the other hand, there are scholars who refer to these situations as re/encounters between the field and the archive or museum (Giordano, 2010, Troya, 2012), which might be more appropriate than repatriation, but, nonetheless, downplays the intentionality implicit in the re/encounter. I therefore opt for using the term *digital return* or simply *return*, which I deem more accurate and less confusing since it refers to the act of a digital piece of cultural heritage being returned either to the people who claim a bond with the material or simply to the "ethnographic site" where it was taken or collected. While the global movement of repatriation of human remains and cultural heritage (in its physical dimension) is at large driven by claims coming from both actors and communities outside and within academia and museums (Nilsson Stutz, 2013), digital returns are most commonly initiated within expert communities and the heritage sector (Bell et al., 2013).

This brings me to discuss the specificity of digital collections depicting both tangible and intangible heritage as opposed to physical museum objects and human remains when it comes to their terms of existence and circulation. While tangible heritage is anchored in the museum storage or exhibition space, digital resources are to be considered highly reproducible and essentially ephemeral (Christen, 2011): They are easily copied and distributed, which allows them to circulate along unexpected routes and exist in multiple locations at once. As opposed to the complex processes involved in the restitution and repatriation of artifacts and human remains stored at museums, the images' reproducible quality, which blurs the boundaries between original and copy, enables multiple ways of sharing without requiring the intervention of the legal system and state authorities. Unlike "cultural" objects, fabricated by subjects that have historically been ethnographized, ethnographic visual collections have almost always been produced by people who don't belong to the portrayed groups. Even if the images weren't in fact produced by the represented groups, there is a certain logic operating and motivating ethnographic returns in which it is assumed that the images "belong" to the communities where they were taken. In this sense, the "ethical" right of the represented subjects coexists with the legal copyright of the author of the image (Edwards, 2003).

Within both approaches there are few studies that look into the ethical implications at stake and the long-term social effects these actions might have on the communities and groups who "receive" the digital return. Although some ethical questions have been addressed such as the need to respect Indigenous protocols of information circulation when facilitating digital access to museum collections (Hennessy, 2009), it still remains uncommon to consider *before* initiating a return the difficult and traumatic past some artifacts, documents or images may represent. Another ethical dimension that should be considered is how our research or the heritage projects we engage with affect the social dynamics in the communities and societies with which we interact (Prins, 2004, Wright, 2009). Here we need to be cautious and not assume that facilitating documents from the past will automatically contribute to conflict-free cultural revitalization processes, the recuperation of endangered languages and the strengthening of traditional knowledge and ceremonies (O'Neal, 2013).

The ethics of ethnographic returns claim a dialogue with a critical approach to heritage in which power relations between different actors and social positioning takes front stage in the analysis. This is in line with the critical turn in heritage studies that stresses the need to interrogate the systems of power implicated in heritage practices and discourse as well as the potential of deploying tangible and intangible heritage to address historical and systematic inequalities (Harrison, 2010, Smith, 2006). It is important to stress that although the act of returning or widening access to ethnographic materials is usually authorized by academics, these actions are carried out in contexts in which groups that have been historically marginalized in heritage practices are constantly asserting and claiming rights to access, interpret and possess their cultural heritage. By inquiring into the needs, interests and values of these communities, it is possible to contrast them with authorized processes of heritage-making, revealing political concerns of diverse stakeholders and contested paradigms of value. Therefore, any ethnographic return needs to be situated in the light of the social and political dimension of heritage and the power relations at work (García Canclini, 1993, Smith, 2006). The conflicts surrounding how heritage is made, labeled, stored, preserved and exhibited, which today involves many actors outside the museum walls, often seem to be downplayed or ignored by a new type of museology that presents itself as communitarian, ethical, memorial and affective (Andermann and Simine, 2012). Paying attention to the political dimension of heritage as well as the meaning production of historically marginalized communities in relation to authorized heritage production is one of the critical components of this study.

1.3 Bridging Gaps between the Archive and the Field

Very few scholars provide reflections on the transition from the institutional heritage domain back to the field, something that can bridge the current gaps between the two existing research approaches. One exception is Elizabeth Edwards (2003), who suggests that these new circulations of images can imply a shift from interpretative regimes that are governed by "public" readings, conditioned by the visual economy upheld by the archive, to other symbolic and experiential frameworks in which more "private" and intimate readings are available, anchored in lived experience or transmitted knowledge. Edwards argues that the traditional constitution of the archive has historically enabled "public" readings of the images preserved there. These are open to multiple interpretations of the cultures represented in the images, but nevertheless operate within a disciplinary paradigm that continually reifies and objectifies the referents in terms of data and archetypes. Unlike this "public" authorized reading of images, in which the meaning is constantly reinterpreted in terms of symbols or metaphors by *outsiders* of the communities that are being represented, images read from an *insider* perspective of intimacy foster ties and affections with the vital domain from which the images were extracted and thereby have the potential to trigger and carry different kinds of memories (Edwards, 2003). This twofold way of understanding ethnographic returns is fundamental to my own research in which I study specific filmic archive images through the lens of shifting symbolic regimes over time as they transit symbolically from a field situation to an institutional sphere and then back to the ethnographic site where they were taken. In order to understand these movements between institutional and affective domains with varying interpretative frameworks, I have adopted a cultural biographical approach (Kopytoff, 1986) in which I reconstruct and study the varying meanings and values attributed to the film throughout its "life" (Mason, 2001), following the traces of its production, circulation in the past, contrasted with the interpretations and "uses" that have emerged during its reception in the present. In this sense, the act of return is only one stage in a much longer cultural biography that is accessed by combining archival research with fieldwork.

With regards to the transition from one domain to the other, this Element tries to comprehend to what extent insider perspectives are capable of decentering and destabilizing the narratives and visual interpretations enabled and upheld by institutional domains such as the archive. I explore how the field speaks back when the flow of information and images between the "archive" and the "ethnographic site" is reverted, looking at how cultural hegemony is articulated in these new readings that are produced outside institutional frameworks.

I argue that to understand the multiple impact and implications of this reversion it is necessary to inquire into the social relations, which enabled not only the production and circulation of the images in the past but also the reception of images in the present. These social relations can also be considered as part of the film's cultural biography. The moment of capture in 1920 and that of reception (in the 2010s) can be seen as different points in time along a longer social process of territorialization (Pacheco de Oliveira, 2019) that is still taking place in the region deeply affecting the people living there. This process involves, among other things, diverse and constantly changing state practices and policies of governability, alterity regimes, as well as the ways subalternized groups respond to these governability efforts and colonizing pressures.

According to this perspective, a visual document produced in a field situation in the past is not only marked by its representational contents and by the values attributed at different moments in its biography, each to be situated in a specific visual economy and symbolic regime, but fundamentally by the social relations that conditioned its capture and circulation in the past and its return in the present. So I set out to interrogate visual objects in terms of their cultural biography, focusing on the contrasts between their lives inside and outside the archive with an emphasis on the social relations that conditioned the different stages in their biography.

Adopting a cultural biographical approach with an emphasis on how social relations condition image-making and consumption required, on one hand, a combination of archival techniques with an ethnographic field approach, and on the other, the articulation of a historical transatlantic study of early film, exploration and settler colonialism – with an ethnographic approach to memory practice as the film is returned in the present-day. In this research I used filmic material shot in 1920 methodologically as a narrative document of the past and at the same time as a way of documenting present memory (Jelin, 2002).

During the screening situations generated during my own fieldwork, both memories and affect and emotions took center stage, making it vital to incorporate and analyze these aspects. This brought my research into dialogue with anthropological approaches in memory studies and discussions concerning the social dimension of emotions. I address memory as a complex articulator of temporalities: as a type of archive, which permits the reconstruction of past events, without underestimating the agency and interests with which people and groups construct their past in the present (Ramos, 2011). In this sense, memory is social practice composed both by profound experiences informed by historical processes, materialities and inherited signification systems and by the hegemonic fields that mark what is possible to remember in the present (Briones, 1994, Ramos, 2011). From this perspective, memory production is to be understood as it changes over time (Hutton, 1993) as something that is dynamically practiced and disputed by groups that don't have the same power to impose their versions of the past as historical truth (Benjamin, 2008 [1940]).

The emergence of affect in the field has called for broadening traditional field techniques such as photo elicitation (Collier, 1957) by combining it with an analysis of the emotional reception of the images. The focus wasn't solely placed on understanding present or past contexts by obtaining ethnographic data and memories based on what was observed in the images. Attention was also paid to the relationship between the comments, silences and gestures during the screenings as well as the perspectives expressed by the viewers as part of complex interpretive frameworks, shaped by historical experience and informed by hegemonic social categories. This way of conceiving affect and emotions builds on interpretative anthropological approaches, in which the social and cultural construction of emotional meaning systems is emphasized (Lutz and White, 1986:420). In my research, I stress how the analysis of emotions and memories registered in the field among historically marginalized communities can contribute to understanding the cross-cultural variations of memory production as well as emotional meaning production in relation to authorized heritage production.

2 "Indians" and "Gauchos" Captured by the Lens of Swedish Explorers in the Argentine Chaco

In this Section, I present the visual archive material I base my research on – namely filmic images shot by Swedish explorer-entrepreneurs with colonizing interests traveling in the Argentine Chaco at the beginning of the twentieth century. This takes place in a context of ongoing conquest and colonization of Indigenous territories carried out and sustained by national state policies (Gordillo and Hirsch, 2003, Lenton, 2010). The film is analyzed as part of a complex transnational history that connects Sweden with South America as well as exploration with early film, settler colonialism and finally also with Nordic anthropology. First, I discuss the initial moment and situation in which the film as a cultural object came into being, focusing on the moment of capture, before it entered into a collecting institution that gave it heritage status. This is followed by showing how the images taken under the entertaining logics of early film pass through a long sinuous process to finally be preserved for future generations as valuable "ethnographic" documentation of the tangible and intangible heritage of "primitive" societies that are seen as on the brink of disappearance.

2.1 Narrating Exploration and Vanishing Life Forms: The Film *Following Indian Trails by the Pilcomayo River*

The black and white nonfiction film *Following Indian trails by the Pilcomayo River* (*På indianstigar vid Pilcomayofloden*, 1950) is today a museum-archive object, but since its "rediscovery" in 2007 has had an active "life" (Mason,

2001) outside its storage at the MWC in Gothenburg, Sweden. It has circulated widely in digital formats throughout Argentina and neighboring countries, awakening great interest among members of Indigenous people as well as historians and anthropologists who study the Gran Chaco region.

This silent[5] film, fifty-minutes long, was released in 1950 by reediting material originally filmed in 1920 during a Swedish expedition to the Pilcomayo River in the Argentine Chaco led by Gustav Emil Haeger.[6] He was accompanied by his assistant, Per Svanbeck, the expedition's photographer and cameraman, Wilhelm Hansson,[7] and Mauricio Jesperson,[8] who was hired as their travel guide. The expedition was driven mainly by commercial interests and was financed solely by its leader, whose family formed part of the rising bourgeoisie linked to the growing paper industry in western Sweden. Haeger sought to study the feasibility of installing colonies and exploiting local natural resources in the Pilcomayo region. The original plan was to cross the Pilcomayo River and explore the Bolivian Chaco, but field circumstances and local inter-tribal conflicts made this impossible. Haeger also aimed to document the expedition visually and to produce footage that could be commercially screened in European movie theaters in the format of travelogues or news reel, as was common in early cinema. He had brought along Hansson for the exclusive purpose of filming and taking photographs. Although not remembered today as an important director in the Swedish film history, Hansson belonged to a reduced group of amateur filmmakers or cameramen who were interested in and could afford to acquire and experiment with this new technology (Hedling and Jönsson, 2007). The expedition also ended up putting together various collections of ethnographic objects as well as taking some entomological samples at the request of the Museum of La Plata, one of the most important Museums in South America at that time.

The biographical data and the nature of the expedition indicate that all four members came from the better standing social classes in Sweden. None of the members had been trained in anthropological or ethnographic methods, and the expedition lacked endorsement or funding from any scientific institution in Sweden. This voyage belongs to a little known tradition of travel to the Chaco carried out by adventurers and entrepreneurs who financed this type of endeavor

---

[5] A silent film is a film with no synchronized sound. The original footage belongs to the silent film period, when it was technically impossible to incorporate sound into moviemaking. See Villarroel (2010).

[6] Haeger held the rank of lieutenant in the *Svea artilleri*, the Swedish Army artillery regiment.

[7] Hansson was also an actor, known for his leading role in Mauritz Stiller's early feature film *The Avenger* (*Hämnaren*, 1915).

[8] Born Mauritz Jesperson in Lund, Sweden, he arrived as a migrant to Argentina in 1913, where he would work and live until the end of the 1930s.

by their own means (Giordano, 2018). Although it was not thought of as a scientific enterprise in itself, the travelers found inspiration in the famous and popularized explorations of the Swedish ethnographer Erland Nordenskiöld who visited the area and in 1910 published a travel account of his encounter with Indigenous tribes along the Pilcomayo River (Gustavsson and Giordano, 2013).

Upon arrival in Buenos Aires, Haeger, Svanbeck and Hansson met Jesperson, a Swede residing in the northern border regions of the country, who would be key in the making of the expedition and film. He was hired by Haeger as the expedition's guide and led them into territories with which he was well acquainted. Jesperson already knew the Pilagá leader Nelagadik, who would eventually allow them to circulate and film in the Indigenous communities. Jesperson was also a good friend of the creole Calermo family who would also be documented visually. This is to say that Jesperson was a key figure in negotiating and obtaining the shots Hansson desired to capture in the field in 1920. As we will see, he also had a leading role in the edition and scriptwriting of the film, which was released in 1950.

In the film *Following Indian Trails by the Pilcomayo River*, a traveler point of view is constructed through the interplay of filmed scenes, intertitles, photographs and maps. Scenes exhibiting the travelers' itinerary and activities are scattered throughout the film, suggesting that as the expedition moves forward, "encounters" with local inhabitants are made. Of the total fifty minutes, two-thirds of the film is exclusively dedicated to portraying the Pilagá, while only seven minutes is used to depict "gauchos" and "creole settlers."[9] Almost all scenes are accompanied by explanatory intertitles in Swedish. The sporadic appearance of maps of Argentina and Chaco make it possible for the public to geographically locate the itinerary of the expedition. Photographs are used to present the Swedish protagonists, the Indian chief Nelagadik – a key figure in negotiating the permission to film the Pilagá – and two images of anonymous Pilagá men. At the end of the film, photographs depict the visual contrast between the travelers' dress and physical appearance in Buenos Aires and in Chaco. In the credits there is a mention of the musical piece "The Inca March," registered by Eric von Rosen in 1902 in Southern Bolivia. During the premiere, this piece was played by a live band,[10] allowing us to presume that the 1950 film was completely silent, although it was technically possible at the time to include sound in a movie production.

---

[9] In the original intertitle in Swedish, they are referred to as "*creolska nybyggare*" and "gauchos."
[10] Press article published on November 28, 1950, "I Chacos urskog för 30 år sedan," *Svenska Dagbladet*.

The narrative structure of the film explicitly celebrates the expedition while simultaneously offering visual and written descriptions of traditional material and immaterial culture. It begins with the explorers' departure on horseback from the last station on one of Chaco's main railway lines, culminates when they reach the Pilagá communities by the Pilcomayo River and ends when the travelers are heading back to the train tracks. The intertitles emphasize their difficult and challenging journey. The title itself *Following Indian Trails by the Pilcomayo River* suggests that it concerns a trip in search of "Indians," which are located far from modern means of transport, to which one can arrive only by following trails. The Gran Chaco is visualized through maps, its geography and climate is described textually as a "green hell," an "impenetrable" place, and ruled by the "hostility of the Indians." After announcing this "harsh" environment, the film shows how the expedition progresses, accomplishing its objectives. In this sense, the film narrates how white male explorers impose their will in adverse circumstances.

The succession of scenes permits the audience to follow the expedition as it moves further away from "civilization." Scenes are combined showing the travelers on horseback as they cross plains, rivers and forests (Figure 1), and the different activities carried out when camping in the wilderness. The hospitality received by the travelers when visiting "creole settlers" is followed by

Figure 1. Explorers crossing the river. Film frame from minute 5:09

Figure 2. Explorers drink mate with the Calermo family. Film frame from minute 9:32

scenes presenting "gauchos" and cattle ranching rodeo activities, as well as different customs and activities related to traditional creole life (Figure 2). The creole settlers are represented by Anselmo Calermo, his wife and children filmed in front of their simple family home. It also documents the rounding up of cattle, as well as how the younger daughters look after the goats and sheep (Figure 3). These scenes, in which the audience is introduced to the topic of travel in the Chaco serve as a preface to the expedition's passage through the "impregnable forests." This is announced by the intertitle "Through the forest the expedition approaches the land of the Pilagá Indians," followed by a map that outlines the journey's itinerary all the way to the "Pilcomayo Indians."

The scene of the expedition members going through the dense vegetation serves as a transition from the known and familiar toward the unknown and different. Suspense is built up and expectations increase with the intertitle "The landscape changes. The palm tree region begins. Finally: on the edge of the forest an Indian village can be seen under huge carob trees." The arrival to the banks of the Pilcomayo unleashes the film's first dramatic climax. While the explorers are filmed when interacting with the creole settlers, they are visually absent in the representation of the Indigenous universe – although at times the script refers directly to their presence and interaction with the Pilagá: "We just

Figure 3. Calermo's daughters with sheep and goats. Film frame from minute
14:06

saw the elders of the tribe smoking. Here the youth experiment with our
Swedish cigarettes."

For twenty-four minutes, ethnographic scenes are combined with descriptive intertitles. After some general pans across the village dwellings, shots show different generations of Pilagá in groups or individually while carrying out crafts (pottery, weapons and textiles) and subsistence activities (fishing, hunting and gathering) or simply posing in front of the camera (Figures 4 and 5). Recreational topics are also included, such as children playing with pets and men engaging in a dice game. In many of these scenes the material culture of the Pilagá is emphasized. For instance, the making of weapons is followed by scenes in which these elements are used to fish. The scenes in which textiles are made are followed by an exhibition of the finished products. The last part is dedicated to ceremonial and festive topics such as the making of the alcoholic beverage *aloja* in relation to the yearly ceremonial gatherings involving dances and chants (Figure 6). In all of these scenes, the camera plays with a variety of shots, using different angles for the same scene, especially close ups when focusing on individuals, but most often using brief shots from a distance, capturing the action of a whole group of people.

During the early period of film, the leading imperial countries – Great Britain, France, the USA and Germany – were major film producers, making the new media at times converge with the promotion of their "colonial projects" (Shohat and Stam, 1994). Lumiére and Edison's cameramen would get on boats and trains, imperial machines, in order to extract "views" of the interiors of Asia, Africa and America to later exhibit them in Europe. These travels undertaken by commercial cameramen were the beginning of multiple forms of cinematographic expeditions that would take place during the early days of cinema.

These early nonfiction films conjugated notions of realism and ethnographic objectivity but also responded heavily to the commercial imperatives of the cinematographic industry on the rise at the time (Griffiths, 1999). Early cinema had its own logic of spectacle: whatever was filmed was turned into spectacle, and collecting filmic images of "native people" and their bodies in movement was popular in early actuality filmmaking (Russell, 2003). Nonetheless, this type of footage brought home from abroad was also attributed certain educational and informational value (Fuhrmann, 2013, Griffiths, 1999, Jernudd, 1999). Actually, during the early years of film, the emerging field of anthropology saw in the cinematograph an objective recording instrument of great potential for the study of primitive culture and society (Grimshaw, 2001, Henley, 2020). However, this enchantment didn't last long. Around the outburst of World War I, ethnographers in the USA and Germany voiced doubts about cinematography's potential in ethnographic observation (Fuhrmann, 2013). In parallel to this scientific short-lasting cinematographic impulse, represented especially by anthropologist Alfred Cort Haddon, a strong film industry was developing that discovered and would come to constantly reinforce a desire to obtain and offer views and travelogues of the distant and exotic.

We are to understand the Swedish film expedition to the Argentine Chaco in the light of these generalized early cinematographic practices related to expanded networks of travel, in which cameramen without any ties to the field of anthropology would shoot and produce ethnographic views for commercial and/or educational purposes. Members of the Swedish well standing social classes indulged eagerly in travel both for purposes of business and pleasure taking advantage of the ever-expanding commercial routes between different continents. At the turn of the century Scandinavia and South America were more connected logistically than ever. The means of transport were rapidly changing, expanding the horizons of travel; making places which once were deemed distant seem closer. As a result of growing trade between Argentina and Sweden, a direct maritime route between Gothenburg and Buenos Aires was inaugurated in 1904, gradually increasing the frequency of departures to one every three weeks.

2.3 Shooting a Film: Social Situation and Negotiations

Although the logic of spectacle pertaining to early film oriented the way the film was shot, the obtained footage was also a result of a series of negotiations that took place in the field. Here I will discuss the social and material conditions and power relations under which these images were taken.

The shooting of the film didn't consist in a quick series of snapshots but rather a two month–long period of negotiated coexistence between subjects belonging to the dominant sectors of society and members of the region's subalternized population. The travelers met up sporadically with the creole Calermo family and some "gauchos"; however, they dedicated most of their time in the field interacting with and visually documenting the Pilagá. As a matter of fact, the shooting became so central to the expedition that the rest of the activities were organized around it. Although the Swedes had their own camp, Hansson's emphasis on filming the Pilagá in their own cultural contexts implied daily excursions to their villages. This resulted in a copresence of filmmaking explorers and filmed subjects during daytime, which was interrupted at night fall when the travelers would retreat to their camp. This daytime copresence that enabled extensive shooting in the Indigenous villages was constantly renegotiated with the Pilagá leaders. The rich archival documentation[13] makes it is possible to gain insight into the social situation in which these permanent negotiations were carried out and provides us with clues as to how the Swedes were perceived by the Indigenous leaders.

In the expedition's field diary, kept by Haeger, it becomes clear that there existed land disputes between the Calermo family and the Pilagá groups. During their stay, the travelers witnessed how Anselmo Calermo had reported to the closest military outpost that he had been threatened by the leader Nelagadik for having trespassed on indigenous fishing ground. Thus, there were rumors of a punitive military expedition organized to punish Nelagadik and his people for their actions against Calermo.

These conflicts registered by the explorers and the expedition's own colonizing interest in the region should be understood in the context of the larger settler expansion in the Argentine Chaco characterized by the incorporation of new lands through military intervention. This expansion was driven by the Argentine

---

[13] I base this on documentation related to the expedition (including correspondence, a field diary, newspaper clippings, movie scripts, etc.) kept at the archive of the MWC in Gothenburg, Sweden. I have also consulted Jesperson's personal papers and documentation, available at the Central Library at Lund University.

state, as well as by regional and foreign capital (Maeder and Gutiérrez, 1995). It was impulsed by military interventions (Beck, 2007),[14] which responded to a settler colonial logic (Veracini, 2010), naturalizing a social order in which the state, the creoles and the European immigrant settlers had the right to colonize the lands inhabited by Indigenous groups. According to this logic, the army's role on this frontier was to protect existing and future settlers like the creole cattle ranchers and European immigrants from the native population. Nonetheless, it is important to highlight that in the Pilcomayo region, where there existed armed Indigenous groups until the 1930s (Gordillo, 2001), the military often sought to establish strategic alliances with certain Indigenous leaders in order to gain insight into territorial dynamics and the localization of different tribes. For instance, until 1919, the Pilagá had cooperated and built "friendly" relations with members of the Argentine army (Sbardella and Braunstein, 1991). When the Pilagá leader Garcete was falsely accused of attacking one of the army's border outposts, these relations were abruptly modified as a wave of state violence was unleashed upon this leader and his people (Vidal and Telesca, In press).

It is in the context of this complex social situation that the Swedes negotiated their daytime presence in the Pilagá villages. The friendly terms of the relations established between the travelers and their filmed subjects were put to the test twice by Pilagá authorities. The explorers were asked to intervene in the conflict between Calermo and Nelagadik, and willingly agreed to write a letter to the military outpost discouraging the punitive expedition. The second request that the Swedes responded to favorably involved a possible armed interethnic conflict between the Pilagá and the Chunupí, one of their traditional enemies. Nelagadik asked the travelers to fight on their side, putting their weapons and equipment at the disposal of the Pilagá. The threat of an attack and the preparations for interethnic warfare were filmed and narrated in the 1950 film. Nonetheless, the documentation related to the expedition contains no evidence of any actual attack.

Up until the 1910s, it was common for Pilagá groups to invite or request explorers and itinerant merchants in the Pilcomayo region to join them in combat against their traditional interethnic war enemies (Bossert and Siffredi, 2011). In 1920, the same type of itinerant actor was not only recruited as an ally against traditional enemies but also against emerging non-Indigenous adversaries who were a fundamental part of the recently constituted social situation. Unlike the military stationed at nearby outposts and the creole cattle ranchers' intrusion on Pilagá grounds for grazing purposes, these foreigners represented

---

[14] M. Matarrese (2013) *Disputas y negociaciones en torno al territorio pilagá (Provincia de Formosa)*. Doctoral dissertation, Facultad Filosofía y Letras Universidad de Buenos Aires (unpublished).

another type of "white"[15] actor who showed no direct threat and was willing to negotiate the terms of a two-month copresence.

The travelers' presence wasn't only negotiated by complying to these specific requests but also by offering work opportunities to members of the village, reproducing labor relations common on sugar cane plantations and factories in northwestern Argentina where many Pilagá migrated each year to carry out seasonal work. Based on Jesperson's knowledge and experience of hiring Indigenous labor, a system of payment for posing or acting in front of the camera was implemented during the shooting. The Indigenous actors were paid with a type of "voucher" made out of reed that could be used to purchase commodities in an improvised trade post set up by the expeditioners. This system made it possible to include many "actors" in the scenes. It is important to point out that staging scenes was common in early film due to the technical limitations of the cinematographs[16] available at the time. Actions were to be carried out in the visual field of the camera and since a shot required preparation it was difficult for the camera to capture spontaneous actions.

In Hansson's cinematographic project, this "staging" was carried out in the Pilagá's own cultural contexts in order to provide "views" as genuine and realistic as possible. Let's recall that the "primitiveness" of Indigenous people was emphasized by the effects of visual realism. In early cinema, Indigenous dances and rituals were often staged in a way that would make them look genuine (Rony, 1996, Russell, 2003). This form of representation insisted on maintaining the filmic fiction that shooting a film didn't alter reality. Hansson went to great efforts to film the Pilagá in their own environment, fundamentally around their own dwellings but also accompanying them to places like the wetlands and riverside where they fished, obtained water and bathed themselves. During the shooting, Jesperson would constantly accompany him, acting as a mediator and translator. The shots were agreed upon with the members of the community in such a way that practices were recreated in situations that corresponded to the expedition's time frame and the requirements of the filmic technology rather than to their customary and ritual sense and purpose.

2.4 From Travelogue and Edutainment to "Ethnographic" Heritage

2.4.1 Early Nonfiction Film in Sweden

Even though a local film industry was flourishing in Buenos Aires in the beginning of the 1920s (Cuarterolo, 2011), once the Swedish travelers returned

---

[15] For how the explorers were seen as "other whites" by Indigenous groups in the Chaco, see Wright (2008).

[16] According to the specialist Douglas Machado (Film Museum "Pablo C. Ducrós Hicken," Buenos Aires), Hansson used a Burke & James Universal camera. For further details on the use of this filmic technology in an expedition context, see Gustavsson (2018b).

to this city from Chaco with rich footage, they showed no interest in exhibiting their films in Argentine theaters. They returned to Sweden with their equipment, colonization studies, maps and a small collection of objects[17] that they had acquired from the Pilagá, as well as photographs and film rolls taken by Hansson. The different colonization projects Haeger had studied and discussed with Jesperson in the field would never be followed up due to his early death in 1921, a few months after returning from Chaco. With the death of its leading figure, the results of the expedition were left to be promoted individually by its members according to their own personal networks, abilities and interests.

The visual results of the expedition started circulating upon Hansson's arrival in Sweden in 1921, presented in various formats to diverse audiences in Europe following logics of commercialization and popularization. Yet, in retrospective they were seen by Hansson himself as a commercial failure (Hansson, 1943). The first editions of the filmic footage were exhibited in short fragmentary formats, as preludes to feature films shown at cinemas in Sweden, Germany, Italy and France (Hansson, 1943). In Sweden, it was common to use nonfiction "views" as preludes to fiction feature film, and by the 1920s there was a growing trend and demand for nonfiction footage depicting both "the nearby and local" as well as "foreign places" (Furhammar, 1991). The filmic footage was also cut and screened as a sixty-minute nonfiction feature film in Stockholm in 1922 under the title *With Stockholmers among Redskins* (*Med stockholmare bland rödskinn*) and also in Finland under the alternative title *Among Indians and Gauchos* (*Bland indianer och gauchos*). Although the actual footage of this edition hasn't been located yet, information about the film's technical characteristics and its contents as well as the place and date of its premiere has been documented.[18] The theater *Victoriasalen* in Stockholm published the following description of *With Stockholmers among Redskins* on the night of its premiere on November 2, 1922:

> Film in four parts about the travels and stays undertaken by a Swedish expedition to a partially unknown region located in the interior of Central South America. 1. Following the paths of travelers in Buenos Aires. 2. Among *gauchos* and cow herds on the Pampa. 3. Through the desert (El Gran Chaco). 4. Visiting the Toba Indians.[19] Brief introductory lecture by the director Vilhelm Hansson including the projection of photographs.

---

[17] These were sent to different Nordic scientific institutions: in 1922 to Carl Vilhelm Hartman at the ethnographic department of the National Museum of Natural History in Stockholm, Sweden, and in 1924 to a colleague of Rafael Karsten at the National Museum of Helsinki, Finland. The remaining objects were donated to the Museum of World Culture of Gothenburg in the 1960s.

[18] Information available at *Svenska Filminstitutets* webpage: www.svenskfilmdatabas.se/en/Item/? type=film&itemid=17445 accessed September 10, 2020.

[19] Calling the Pilagá "Toba" in a nordic context might be due to the fact that, unlike the Pilagá, the Toba, who also lived in the Pilcomayo region, had been studied by Finnish anthropologist Rafael Karsten in the 1910s.

Although it isn't possible to actually see the film and analyze its narrative structure, its division into four parts suggests that the brief films and "views" taken during the expedition and edited under the logics of actualities were here integrated into a more extensive narrative sequence overcoming a fragmented mostration of "loose" scenes.

I suggest that Hansson's nonfiction feature film can be understood in relation to other Swedish contemporary nonfiction motion pictures produced in expedition contexts, forming part of a transition of nonfiction cinema toward more narrative forms. This transition coincided with the emergence of edutainment, a new filmic genre that fused entertainment with education, seen as a vehicle to educate children as well as the masses of workers (Jernudd, 1999). Films such as *Among Savages and Wild Beasts* (*Bland vildar och vilda djur*, 1921), fifty five–minutes long, and *On Safari in Africa with Prince Wilhelm* (*Med prins Wilhelm på afrikanska jaktstigar*, 1922), fifty-minutes long, both shot by Oscar Olsson during his expeditions to Central Africa, constitute not only milestones in this transition but also exemplify how films originally meant to entertain could be merged with educational values (Jernudd, 1999). Nonetheless, even though the narrative connects one "view" with the next through the insertion of intertitles uniting bits and pieces within an overarching story line, Jernudd notes that in these motion pictures, the logics of monstration prevail. Hansson's films seem to have undergone a similar process of editing and "sewing" together fragmentary views. Thus, it is possible to suppose the predominance of "actuality" and newsreel logics in the production as well as in the distribution of Hansson's films, even when the documentation points to a certain degree of experimentation with longer narrative structures.

2.4.2 Illustrating Travel Lectures and Scientific Events

Although the first movie theater in Sweden opened in 1907, many films were shown before and after this year, especially at places related to social movements such as the sobriety movement and Free Churches (Hedling and Jönsson, 2007). Hansson used many of these types of venues to speak about the expedition. So not only did his films circulate in shorter and longer formats in movie theaters but were also potentially shown accompanying the lectures he held at associations, study circles, schools and clubs in Sweden and Finland (Hansson, 1943).

One of the exhibition formats of early film available outside movie theaters was accompanied by lectures told by travelers who had experienced personally what was being shown in the projected images. This type of exhibiting practice was carried out by "travelling lecturers," such as the American Burton Holmes

(1870–1958), as part of recreation and entertainment activities in urban contexts both in the USA and Great Britain between 1897 until the 1920s (Griffiths, 1999). Although in Sweden there are no studies on this type of itinerant exhibitions, Hansson's illustrated lecturers about the expedition have many points of contact with the traveling lecturer practice. Nonetheless, in the Swedish context, these exhibiting lectures seem to have taken place in spaces related to social movements and popular education rather than those pertaining to recreational activities.

Hansson was also invited to exhibit his visual production at scientific events organized by the Nordic anthropological community. In 1925, he presented "a film which was shot during Haeger's expedition to Gran Chaco"[20] at the Swedish Society for Anthropology and Geography in Stockholm. The film was exhibited after a conference given by anthropologist Rafael Karsten about his own expedition to Ecuador where he carried out fieldwork among various ethnic groups. Hansson and Karsten had met personally the year before in Helsinki, when a few ethnographic objects from Haeger's expedition were donated to the National Museum in that city.[21] Although the conference was about Indigenous people in Ecuador, Karsten was familiar with the Pilcomayo region filmed by Hansson. Both Karsten and fellow ethnographers Erland Nordenskiöld and Eric von Rosen had carried out anthropological research in the Gran Chaco in the 1910s, turning this region into one of Nordic Americanism's primary field sites in South America. This may be one of the reasons Hansson's visual productions were interesting to Karsten. Actually, a decade later, Karsten included photographs taken during Haeger's expedition in one of his publications on Chaco tribes (Karsten, 1932). In the epigraphs, the Pilagá were described as "tobas from the argentine Chaco." Since Karsten hadn't been able to take high-quality photographs himself during his fieldwork in 1911–1913 among the Chorotes of the Pilcomayo and the Tobas of Villa Montes, Bolivia, he used pictures obtained by other expeditions in neighboring areas to illustrate his research (Salomaa, 2002). All this suggests that the ethnographic quality of Hansson's films and photography was recognized by certain members of the Nordic anthropological community. The way he depicted Indigenous life in the Chaco in its own cultural contexts could both entertain as well as illustrate scientific events and publications.

---

[20] As described in the newspaper article published in 1925, "Professor Karsten om sina studier av indianernas religion," *Stockholms tidningen*, consulted at the Central Library in Lund University.

[21] See correspondence between Gunnar Haeger and Rafael Karsten and a letter to Anna Haeger, signed by Professor U. T. Sirelius at the ethnographic department of the National Museum in Helsinki. Documentation consulted at the MWC archive.

2.4.3 Constructing Ethnographic Narrative

In the 1940s, the filmic material was restudied and finally turned into the fifty minute–long film *Following Indian Trails by the Pilcomayo River,* starting the second period of circulation and reception that forms part of its cultural biography. This new period was activated as a joint project between two of the expedition's members. When Jesperson returned to Sweden in the 1940s he met up with Hansson, and they initiated this reedition project, counting on the financial support of Gunnar Haeger, the deceased expedition leader's brother. The making of a new film based on the original footage was undertaken through a type of scriptwriting by which the visual narrative was given structure. The script organized and systematized the "views" and scenes that had been filmed in 1920 by giving them order and adding explanatory intertitles. After Hansson's sudden death in 1948, Jesperson finished the reedition by himself, becoming the film's main promoter and scriptwriter. It was finally screened in a gala context organized by the Swedish Argentine Association with the participation of the Swedish Chaco Travelers' Association at the high-society venue *Stallmästargården* in Stockholm, its main audience being the members of these associations.

This version of the film, the only one which has been preserved, combines narrative elements common in expedition film with those pertaining to ethnographic documentaries – the latter having been established by the 1940s as a nonfiction film genre. By this time, the Indigenous people of South America had become a common topic in documentaries and fiction films.[22] As common in this newly established genre, the film contains two enunciation modes – that of *monstration* and *narration* (Gaudreault, 1987). The first one contains micronarratives that emerge during the shooting, upon which a longer more englobing narrative is established through the editing process. In the case of this film, the micronarratives are inscribed in Hansson's cinematographic practice as negotiated in the field, while the macronarrative, elaborated thirty years after the shooting, is based on Jesperson's scriptwriting and editing, inspired by travel writing and ethnographic description (Gustavsson and Giordano, 2013).

If we were to compare Hansson's 1922 film edition with the 1950 edition, we can only infer from the written description of the first one that the latter contained more scenes depicting the Indigenous population. In 1922, only one act out of four was dedicated to the "Toba," while in 1950, two-thirds of the film was exclusively dedicated to narrating Pilagá customs and material culture. Once the macronarrative and edition was defined by Jesperson, the Pilagá were

---

[22] G. Carreño (2007) *Miradas y alteridad. La imagen del indígena latinoamericano en la producción audiovisual.* Masters dissertation, Universidad de Chile (unpublished).

turned into the main subjects of the film. The ethnographic value of the film was also emphasized, not only by inserting precise textual explanations of what was seen in the scenes but also by declaring in the script's closing lines that the Pilagá customs and practices seen in the movie had vanished in the 1930s. This new mode of *narration* was also sustained and legitimized by Jesperson's increasing recognition as a Swedish authority on the Chaco region.

Jesperson was deeply informed by his long-standing personal experience in the Chaco. By the time he returned to Sweden, he had lived for over twenty years in the Argentine Chaco, having founded his own cattle farm in the area explored in 1920 and administrated a creole settler colony in the Pilcomayo region for over ten years (Gustavsson, 2016). By the end of the 1940s, he had acquired a literary voice and had become a public figure thanks to various autobiographical novels he published about his adventures in Argentina (Jesperson, 1941, 1942, 1943a), his frequent participation in radio shows and the subsequent media coverage. He also published a text with ethnographic ambitions, describing some aspects of Pilagá society and culture (Jesperson, 1943b). This amateur ethnographic description was never reviewed nor commented upon by members of the anthropological community, but can be seen together with the scriptwriting as a way to establish himself as a Swedish expert on the region and to make sure Haeger's expedition and his own travels across Gran Chaco be included in the Swedish travel tradition to the region. As cofounder of the Swedish Chaco Travelers' Association, he was also well aware of the interest and nostalgia Chaco inspired in some circles of high society in Stockholm, especially among members of the elite who had traveled to Chaco in their youth.

2.4.4 Heritage-Making and Ethnographic Film Archives

Although the 1950 film announced the vanishing of the "primitive" life forms shot in 1920, the anthropological community and the institutions dedicated to storing, studying and exhibiting ethnographic heritage in Sweden hesitated in attributing it scientific value. In this second period of the images' lives, their circulation and reception were strongly limited to circles pertaining to the Swedish high society with prominent roles in commercial and diplomatic relations with Argentina, in some cases with direct experience of travel and exploration of the Chaco. It was only in the 1960s, with the increasing valorization of ethnographic film in Swedish ethnographic museums, that the film was acquired by one of these institutions. This heritage-making process, although slow and bumpy, is what finally confirmed the film's status as "ethnographic," guaranteeing its store and preservation until today.

Let's examine the private gala context in which the film was premiered in Stockholm in 1950. The event was covered by four of the main newspapers of the time,[23] with a general focus on describing the social dimension of the event rather than caring to make a critique of the film. There was no mention of the film's potential ethnographic or scientific value. The gathering included those who usually attended the annual events organized by the Swedish Argentine Association, this time also coupled by members of Swedish Chaco Traveler's Association, created in 1941. Many guests had commercial and diplomatic ties to Argentina and Sweden, such as the director of the Swedish company Aktiebolaget Gasaccumulator (AGA) and representatives from Standard Oil, as well as from the governments of Argentina and Uruguay and the Swedish foreign affairs office. The guests who had some kind of relation to Chaco reflected a very broad and varied travel tradition between Sweden and this region of South America. It included those who had searched for oil in the region on the account of Standard Oil, men who had worked with colonizing enterprises such as Jesperson and those who had tried their luck navigating the Pilcomayo River. Members of the scientific and academic community were largely absent, except for Robert Fries who had participated in the Chaco Cordillera expedition run by the well-known Americanist Erland Nordenskiöld and the Countess Mary von Rosen, wife to the late Eric von Rosen who had participated in the same expedition.

Although, one of the main themes of the evening was the celebration of the thirtieth anniversary of Haeger's expedition, the speeches held by the authorities of the associations also spoke of other matters of importance to the Swedish-Argentine community. Nonetheless, Jesperson was one of many protagonists who gave an introductory lecture before the screening of the film. The fact that the premiere took place in this highly commemorative atmosphere can be seen as an effort to inscribe not necessarily the film but rather the expedition in the memory of the Swedish-Argentine community and in the historiography of Swedish traveling and exploration.

This rich press material and the fact that this private social gathering was the only documented screening occasion gives us insight into not only the high society and elitist profile of the audience who actually viewed the film but also indicates the type of audience Jesperson had in mind when writing the script and reediting the footage. Although the existence of two original scripts, one in Spanish and one in English, suggests that screenings for Spanish-speaking audiences might have been intended,

---

[23] Press articles published the day after the social event on Tuesday November 28, 1950: (1) "Gräshopparnas land," *Aftonbladet*; (2) Sive, "Trettioårig film från Gröna Helvetet premiärvisas för Gran Chaco-farare," *Dagens Nyheter*; (3) "I Chacos urskog för 30 år sedan," *Svenska Dagbladet*; (4) Gala-Peter, "Gästabud," *Expressen*.

there is no other documentation that supports such an assumption. Years later, in 1971, some scenes from the film would be presented on Swedish television (SVT) as part of a series of programs titled "Swedish expeditions,"[24] in which writer and filmmaker Rolf Blomberg presented Haeger's expedition through its filmic production, situating it within a wider Swedish travel tradition to South America that included anthropologists such as Nordenskiöld and travel writers such as himself. Although the screening of fragments of the film in this television context surely reached a broader audience than the 1950 premiere, on both occasions the general narrative accompanying the filmed scenes emphasized the heroic role of exploration rather than the richness of the ethnographic register.

Before its grand gala premiere in 1950, Hansson's wife had offered a copy of the film to the Ethnographic Museum in Stockholm. In a letter[25] to her signed by anthropologist Gerhard Lindblom, who was at the time director of this museum, he expressed how glad he was that Hansson's film had finally been reedited, allowing it to be "presented in the worthy conditions it deserves, as a documentary film without unnecessary cutting and 'popularizing' in the worst sense of this last word." This comment presents an interesting view on film; it indicates that filmic footage generated in an expedition context and originally screened as popular entertainment could acquire scientific value when reedited into another more "serious" format such as the documentary. In the letter, Lindblom also stated that although he personally didn't know whether the Pilagá still maintained some of their ancient culture, he considered that since the film was recorded such a long time ago, the material "must surely be of great scientific interest" and that acquiring a copy of the film would "be of interest to the state's ethnographic museum." Nevertheless, he explained that the institution at the time had no financial means to acquire the material. In Lindblom's response, it becomes clear that the museum's commitment in the form of financial resources was with material culture, in the form of collections of ethnographic objects.

Here we see how a prominent anthropologist attributed scientific value to the film based not only on its potential to show a culture that had partially or completely disappeared but also on its new "worthier" format and edition. Nonetheless, although classifiable as a documentary of scientific value, there was a certain reluctance to perceive the filmic register as a type of heritage worth preserving as per se in an ethnographic museum.

Twelve years later, in 1962, Gunnar Haeger approached the Museum of World Culture in Gothenburg (at the time called "Gothenburg Museum of

---

[24] The specific program in which footage from the expedition was shown held the title "Swedish Expeditions: On Indian Trails in Chaco 2," broadcast on March 13, 1971 on SVT1. The program is stored at the audiovisual archive at the Royal Library in Stockholm, Sweden.

[25] Letter from Lindblom to Matti Hansson, dated March 1, 1950, MWC Archive.

Ethnography") wishing to donate a collection of Pilagá objects, which had been collected by his deceased brother during the expedition and which had been in the family for over forty years. It is in this context and under the definition of a collection's "associated documentation" that Hansson's filmic footage finally enters a heritage holding institution. In a letter to Haeger, anthropologist Henry Wassén, who was at the time curator at the museum, confirms the objects' official entry into the museum's collections, and how some of the donated documentation had been associated to the collection. With regards to the filmic material, Wassén seemed puzzled about how to name and store it: "I still haven't found the moment to take care of it, nor have I gained clarity in what the museum can do with the films (or film?), which must have pure documentary value for the other [collection]."[26] The concern expressed by Wassén in his letter with regards to the care and definition of film in plural or singular indicates that he was unsure when a new type of materiality was to be entered into a system of classification and storage that hadn't previously considered such material as part of the institution's heritage. In the case of the Museum of World Culture of Gothenburg, this resistance to conceive of the film as ethnographic heritage is overcome in 1968 with the museum's official creation of an ethnographic film archive (Wassén, 1970), in which *Following Indian Trails by the Pilcomayo River* is the first film to appear in the newly created record. The reasons for creating such an archive were anchored in the idea that "the worth of a film archive for an ethnographic museum is as obvious for documentation purposes as that of a discography archive" (Wassén, 1970:55), suggesting an increasing valorization and institutionalization of sonorous and visual recordings of "exotic" immaterial culture in the Swedish museum context.

As the film is incorporated into the museum's heritage, the explorers' gaze and voices become part of an institutional authorized heritage discourse. The ethnographic authority constructed through the script of the film is also confirmed and enhanced. By entering the ethnographic paradigm of value, the previous stages in the object's biography, linked to logics of edutainment and colonizing interests, are overshadowed. Wassén's emphasis on its documentation value also indicates how the heritage-making process turns the visual material into a public document on the history of the region and its population.

3 Readings of the Past and the Affective Reception of an Archive Film

In this Section, I will discuss a new period in the "lives" of these images, triggered by returning them in the twenty-first century to the places where they were shot.

---

[26] Letter from Wassén to Gunnar Haeger, dated March 17, 1962, MWC archive.

I reflect upon the conditions of this return, my own role in the endeavor and how the film has been valued, used and interpreted in these places today by different publics. I base myself on my fieldwork there, which included generating specific screening events and workshops on the topic, as well as participating in religious and political events and engaging in everyday activities and conversations.

Unlike most literature on digital and visual returns, I address the archival images and their reception in two different publics, representing two culturally differentiated social groups that have maintained asymmetric relationships with each other for over 100 years: members of the Pilagá Indigenous people and creole cattle ranchers who participated as settlers in the historical dispossession of the Pilagá. As will be seen, the historical construction of whiteness, creoleness and indigeneity in the Argentine Chaco has conditioned the way I have been able to define publics and carry out screening activities in the field. These constructions of difference together with each collective's specific historical experience inform the memory practices, emotional meaning systems and interpretative frameworks with which the images are currently interpreted and valued in Formosa.

3.1 Locating and Defining Audiences

3.1.1 Tracing Social Categories

Since the film represents both creoles and Pilagá, I have inquired into how these categories work in defining social relations and social belonging in contemporary Formosa. When I initiated my fieldwork, I wondered in what circumstances, how and by whom these terms became relevant when referring to Formosa's present population. This included finding out how these categories had been constructed historically and how they could be used hegemonically in the present to mark social inclusion and exclusion as well as to reframe ethnic self-demarcations (Briones, 2004).

To identify the people or groups who recognize themselves in these terms was far easier in the case of the Pilagá, who became officially recognized by the Province of Formosa as one of four Indigenous people in 1984 when the "Aboriginal Integral law"[27] was sanctioned. This process in which the rights of various Indigenous people of Formosa were recognized opened a new phase in their relations with the Argentine state, which has historically been characterized by both extermination and tutelage practices, first on behalf of the national government and, since 1955,[28] the provincial one. Thanks to this

---

[27] In Spanish it is called *Ley Integral del Aborigen 426/84.*

[28] The province of Formosa was created in 1955. Before this date, it was considered a national territory, administered by the national government.

legal framework, most Pilagá currently live on communally owned land plots in peri-urban and rural areas,[29] spread out over the center of the province (Spadafora et al., 2010). Some families have also migrated to larger towns and cities in the region and to other provinces (Vivaldi, 2016).

It is worth mentioning that since the Pilagá were captured by Hansson's lens in 1920, they have been intensively ethnographized. Thanks to ethnographic studies carried out by Swiss ethnologist Alfred Métraux (1937, 1946a) and Argentine anthropologist Enrique Palavecino (1928, 1933), this seminomadic ethnic group became known to the anthropological community from the 1930s. Since then, they have been studied from various approaches and theoretical-methodological frameworks (e.g., Dell Arcipete, 1991, Henry and Henry, 1944, Idoyaga Molina, 1996, Newbery, 1983, Sbardella and Braunstein, 1991).[30] The outcome has been not only a wide range of literature about their traditional myths and culture and historical experience but also a double marking process in which the "ethnic othering" of the Pilagá has been reinforced throughout the twentieth century, both by academia and State policies.

The Pilagá have undergone complex sedentarization and evangelization processes since the expedition took place and the first ethnographies were published. The evangelization processes have been studied in great depth by various anthropologists who assert that for the Pilagá and other Indigenous peoples of Gran Chaco, the adoption of Christian religiosities (Catholic, Anglican, Mormon and Evangelical) has resulted in the emergence of a syncretic spirituality in which shamanic and Christian elements are combined (Citro, 2009, Cordeu and Siffredi, 1971, Miller, 1979, Wright, 2008). In the case of the Pilagá, this new syncretized form of spirituality appeared first in the 1940s with a messianic movement that was later canalized and absorbed especially by the pentecostal *Iglesia Evangélica Unida*, the first autonomous Indigenous church in Argentina, through systematic incorporations into what locally is referred to as the *evangelio* (Vuoto, 1986). This has led to the creation and persistence of numerous churches in the Pilagá communities, led by Indigenous leaders.

When it comes to the Pilagá's sedentarization process, the picture is less clear. It can be seen as one of the outcomes of a more generalized territorialization process that restricted their mobility, limiting hunting, fishing and gathering practices, making the communities depend to a greater extent on the seasonal migrations in search of work on estates related to the sugarcane and forestry

---

[29] In 2007, twenty-three Pilagá communities had been formed. In order to be granted communally owned land titles, each community created a civil association that would serve as a liaison with the state-run agency called *Instituto de Comunidades Indígenas* (ICA).

[30] See note 14.

industries (Gordillo, 2004), on simple, informal and sporadic work in the towns, or on agricultural activities in their own communities. According to Matarrese,[31] this process intensified at the end of the 1940s, after the Rincón Bomba massacre. This is an episode of state violence and extermination during which hundreds of Pilagá men, women and children were brutally executed by the Argentine security forces (Mapelman, 2015). The massacre reformulated the conditions of domination and subjugation between the Pilagá and the Argentine state, marking an inflexion in their traditional mobility and territoriality. From successfully managing to avoid being incorporated into the missions and state-owned reductions created for assimilation purposes in the first half of the twentieth century (Métraux, 1946b), post-massacre, after an initial territorial dispersion, the surviving families returned to the lands located at a considerable distance from the towns, negotiating with the national government tools and land titles for agricultural purposes (Coquero, 1999).

As discussed in the previous section, the term *"creole"* appeared as a "social type" in the film and in the written documentation related to the expedition, but was far harder to track as an expression of social belonging during my fieldwork. Although existing as a denomination for a portion of Formosa's population dedicated to cattle ranching (Beck, 2007), the creoles (*criollos* in Spanish) have been of little interest to historians specializing in northeastern Argentina. Nor have they received the attention of the local anthropological tradition, which has been solely devoted to the study of Indigenous people living in Chaco (Abduca et al., 2014).

However, through my research I have found that the cattle ranchers who colonized the region at the outset of the twentieth century have historically held marginal positions in relation to the dominant sectors of society. Together with environmental factors, this marginality has resulted in severe restrictions on their original transhumance practices. At the beginning of the 1970s, the Pilcomayo River retreated upriver, causing, on one hand, the drying up of large extensions of the main riverbed, and, on the other, provoked the flooding of an area in central Formosa that would eventually turn into a permanent wetland known as *Bañado La Estrella*[32] (Gordillo, 2001). Since the *Bañado* became an optimal area for cattle ranching where much of this activity was concentrated, this transformed the creole transhumance practices that had been characterized until then by the crossing of large extensions of northwest and central Formosa, following the course of the Pilcomayo River and crossing over to Paraguay and Bolivia. In addition to this, those cattle ranchers who had

---

[31] See note 14.

[32] These wetlands cover approximately 400,000 hectares, covering parts of western and central Formosa.

occupied state-owned *Bañado* lands were forced to adopt the measures implemented by the provincial government since its creation in 1955 that aimed to
regulate the land tenure system. The gradual selling off and formalization of
land possession also contributed to restricting territorially cattle ranching
activities.

Although marginalized and restricted territorially, the cattle ranching creoles
have not been ethnically marked by the state in the Formosan context. Unlike
the Pilagá, they have not suffered the same type of violence nor have they been
forcefully dispersed and regrouped in the territory. Even though at times whole
families partook in transhumance practices, the women and children often
remained in one place, settling down in different spots called *parajes* that
were scattered throughout the rural areas. This gradual sedentarization process
was not controlled and monitored by the state as was the case with their
ethnically marked neighbors. Another important point is that these cattle ranchers were, although mobile, a major colonizing force in the Pilcomayo region
where the Pilagá had their traditional hunting and fishing grounds at the beginning of the twentieth century, thereby participating in the process of dispossession of Indigenous lands.

This contrasting situation between the two filmed groups as well as their
historical antagonism had an impact on my field entry and on the identification
of potential audiences for the screenings. During my fieldwork, I noticed that
this sharp contrast in historical experience, especially in relation to ethnic
othering processes, profoundly informed each collective's present interpretation frameworks and affective ties to the past.

3.1.2 Field Entry

I will start by describing how I got in touch with members of the Pilagá
communities. Through a local nongovernmental organization (NGO),[33] in
2013 I contacted the Indigenous organization *Federación Pilagá*[34] (from here
on *Federación*), which represents 90 percent of the officially recognized Pilagá
communities in Formosa. Since its foundation at the beginning of the 2000s, it
has been attempting to construct autonomous Indigenous representation outside
of the provincial party political machinery, trying to cut down on the dependency between Indigenous community representatives and provincial state actors
(Spadafora et al., 2010).

---

[33] This NGO is dedicated to the development of Indigenous communities in central Formosa and is
part of a larger network of organizations with a strong Christian-oriented base that has been
present in this province since the 1960s. See Leone (2019).

[34] The formal name of the organization is *Federación de comunidades indígenas del Pueblo
Pilagá*, which means Federation of Indigenous Communities Pertaining to the Pilagá People.

Over the following years, I built up a relationship with the elected members of the *Federación* and followed its development and struggles. Its members supported my research, provided me with their own accounts of the importance of the material that had been returned and even used the filmic material on a few occasions. They urged me to write a book on Pilagá history stemming from my research that could be used by Indigenous teachers, and put me in contact with relevant people. This has led to a number of encounters and workshops with bilingual intercultural teachers and community representatives in which visual and written archive material was discussed and at times became confronted by memory practices. This is how the political emergence of the Pilagá in Formosa and their politics of memory became central in understanding counter-hegemonic narratives of the past when discussing the archive material.

In parallel, I also pursued a second field entry that enabled me to discuss the material with Indigenous preachers, evangelical musicians and community leaders in rural communities who weren't actively involved in supporting Indigenous autonomy outside of state administration networks.

Much harder was the task of identifying and localizing audiences related to the so-called creole settlers of 1920. At first, I thought the hegemonic sectors of Formosa society recognized themselves as creole but soon found out that there was much ambiguity around the idea of being "white" and/or "creole."

Through small talk and by asking around in the town center of Las Lomitas, located in the center of the province, I met various residents who recognized their creole roots without identifying themselves as such. All of them were born in the Pilcomayo River region (present border region between Argentina and Paraguay) and had for different reasons in the middle of the twentieth century migrated south to the towns that had developed and grown in size along the railway line. They held different social positions; some were well off, having turned into shopkeepers and bar owners, while others had continued as rural workers although they lived in an urban context. A third group had not been forced to migrate to the cities but had moved their families to an urban context for the sake of their children's education, while still maintaining lands with cattle ranch activity in the *Bañado*.

I was told by these residents that the "true" creoles lived in the rural areas surrounding the towns and cities. According to one of the founders of *Asociación de Productores del Bañado La Estrella* (APROBAE), an organiza-tion active between 2004 and 2010 that represented the interests of cattle ranchers from the *Bañado* who had been affected by the construction of a provincial route (Beck, 2010), the creoles constitute an impoverished rural population that combine cattle ranching with other small-scale productive activities. The families who hadn't migrated to the larger towns lived in small villages called *parajes* but most often their ranches were scattered over the rural space, being more or less remote from the rural Indigenous communities. When I undertook my fieldwork, this rural population that was defined by a shared economic activity had no active organization that represented them or brought them together. APROBAE was dissolved once the road conflict had been resolved.

Given my limited mobility in difficult-to-access rural areas, I could only access a few residences. Therefore, I decided to study the reception of the film with inhabitants of Las Lomitas who had a strong link to the Pilcomayo area, including people who claimed that they were direct descendents of the creole protagonists in the film. I thus constituted an audience that perceived themselves as "urban" and "white," while at the same time recognizing a rural origin and creole ancestry.

Regarding the relation between the rural and urban space, it is interesting to note that for the residents of Las Lomitas who recognize their creole roots, the migration of their families to this town has meant an abrupt end to their rural experience. In the case of the Pilagá, many of whom have settled down in the periurban communities outside the towns of Las Lomitas and Pozo del Tigre, there is a constant mobility between the towns and the communities located in rural areas. This constant circulation is motorized by the visits to relatives living in different communities and the participation in social and religious festivities organized by the Indigenous evangelical churches. Besides, every month, members of the rural communities travel to the towns to run different errands, collect social benefits, visit the hospital and buy provisions.

3.2 Alterity Formation and Memory Practices in the Argentine Chaco

Here I introduce the specific way that the Argentine nation-state has produced and still produces its "internal others" (Briones, 2004), following a historical construction of "alterity" that informed the solutions to the "Indian problem" at the time the explorers were shooting their film and that even today permeates the matrix of relations and identifications in this region where "whites" and "creoles" are clearly differentiated from the Indigenous population called "aborigines." These categories have been key to understanding the social positions and identifications from which the film is read and interpreted in the present. Since the film is recognized as representing the past, I also analyze how and by which means different aspects of the past, seen or unseen in the film, are mobilized and disputed from specific social positions and identity ascriptions in the present.

3.2.1 National Formation of Alterity and Regional Territorialization Processes in Argentina

As of the end of the nineteenth century, nation-building forces were operating on a large scale throughout Latin America. Amongst other things, this implied the configuration of different national formations of alterity (Segato, 1998), which nurtured and were nurtured by state practices of extermination and tutelage toward a number of "internal others." These practices responded to the diverse interests that the economic and political powers of the young republics had in the territories that were still under the control of Indigenous groups (Pacheco de Oliveira, 2019).

In contrast to other nation-building projects in Latin America, the constitution of Argentina as a nation-state follows a settler colonial logic (Veracini, 2010), combining systematic attempts to eliminate, silence and assimilate its Indigenous population with a strong promotion of European immigration through state policies. In this particular national formation, various regions that were to be incorporated into the nation-building project were called "deserts" (Halperín Donghi, 1982, Wright, 2008). These geographies, where the Indigenous population was resisting the advance of the state, were understood by the Euro-American elites as the opposite of "civilization," as spaces lacking state control and economic productivity in need of radical transformations (Wright, 2008), ultimately justifying a long series of military interventions against the native populations. On the bases of these acts of military conquest, accompanied by discourses that affirmed the extermination of the rebellious natives, the Indigenous component came to occupy an ambiguous place in the national imaginings. As many authors (Briones, 2005, Gordillo and Hirsch, 2003) have pointed out, in relation to this assault on the "desert," the dominant narratives have historically emphasized the homogeneity, Europeanness and whiteness of the nation, although not completely being able to erase its Indigenous composition. Not only would the "conquered" Indigenous population gain attention and a certain type of visibility through the policies developed by provincial and federal state agencies to administrate the country's "internal others" throughout the twentieth century (Lenton, 2010), but also constitute an unrecognized and vanishing yet culturally productive presence in the national imaginings (Lazzari, 2003).

Emphasizing the nation's whiteness has left little room for celebrating the Indigenous as well as the *mestizo* component of the nation, in clear contrast with other Latin American countries such as Mexico, Brazil or Peru (Gordillo and Hirsch, 2003). This particular national formation of alterity has allowed, and at times made compulsory, a whitening process by which the Indigenous and afro-descendent populations have been encouraged to "dilute" their ethnic markers by choosing to identify with their least stigmatized ancestor (Briones, 2002).

This national formation of alterity needs to be understood in articulation with regional processes of territorialization and localized constructions of social categories that involved contrasting settling strategies, productive models and state policies, designed to deal with the "Indian problem." The specific system of economic production and exploitation developed in Chaco entailed particular forms in which the populations demarcated as Indigenous were disciplined, subjugated and at times even exterminated. In Chaco and northwestern Argentina, the sugarcane and cotton industries were labor intensive and required an available sedentary and productive population that could provide the sector with cheap labor (Gordillo, 2004). The latter gave rise to systematic attempts at sedentarizing the Indigenous population by gathering them in reductions, missions and reserves.

In relation to these economic interests, the military interventions in the region were meant to "pacify" rather than exterminate the "indians." It was assumed that it was possible for the Indigenous population to assimilate into Western society and capitalist relations of production (Lenton, 1997, Lois, 2001). Thus, in the campaign to the north, the natives were disciplined and subjugated by the military forces, in an attempt to convert them into the labor force that the regional industries required. One of the strategies used consisted of depriving the Indigenous people of their territories, limiting their economies based on hunting, gathering and trade activities, thus forcing them to become wage earners (Gordillo, 2004).

3.2.2 Social Categories and Hegemonic Memory Practices in the Argentine Chaco

The image of Formosa as a society socially divided into whites, creoles and aborigines[35] showed up constantly during conversations with both Indigenous and non-Indigenous interlocutors. These hegemonic categories of demarcation and self-demarcation (Briones, 2004) are the building blocks with which identifications are constructed in this region within the parameters established by Argentina's specific national formation of alterity. However, although they are shared categories, let's be reminded that the dominant sectors of society who define themselves explicitly as "white" with possible creole ancestry and roots

---

[35] Although the word *"indígena"* exists in Spanish, in Formosa the Indigenous population has been referred to historically as *"aborígenes,"* a term that is symbolically associated with a series of negative attributes.

produce and update the historical formation of alterity, which shapes the hegemonic stigmatizing sense of aborigine (Gordillo, 2004).

On various occasions, during my conversations with a lady around sixty-five-years old who owns the town's first pharmacy, she used the category "white" to differentiate herself from the "aborigines" who she claimed were the "typical inhabitants" of the region: "The aborigine is typical, the typical character among the first inhabitants … they don't 'mix' much with the whites … Them aborigines and us whites, although nowadays they are a bit more integrated. There are people that take it upon them to integrate them."

To speak in terms of "them aborigines and us whites" shows how natural it is to ethnically demarcate a portion of the population as aborigine, simultaneously reinforcing indigeneity as the opposite of whiteness. This phrasing of words isn't exceptional but rather the generalized demarcation categories that nurtures the way the dominant sectors define themselves when faced by Indigenous alterity. They are referred to as "first inhabitants," which implies the recognition of their preexistence. Nonetheless, their social and cultural contribution to the present-day society is seen as nonexistent. Although the provincial and national legal framework establishes the right of the Indigenous people to their culture and language, the representatives of the traditional families still refer to a gradual and tutored "integration" process by which the aborigines are to enter a society defined and measured in terms of the dominant sectors of society. This view of a progressive integration also entails leaving behind them the extreme poverty that indigeneity has been associated with historically in the regional formation of alterity (Gordillo, 2004).

All the same, stressing whiteness and using "white" as an identity category is not only activated to mark distance from ethnic otherness but also from a creole past associated with rural life and poverty. The creoles are simultaneously described as natives and first or original inhabitants. It is interesting to note that in various authorized written narratives about Formosa's past, the Indigenous population as well as the creoles are brought together in a preurban original temporality, existing before the foundation of the towns along the railroad line: "The initial inhabitants were the *originarios*,[36] including different ethnic groups as well as some creoles" (Arce Bazán, 2013:26). These written narratives, representing an official and authorized local history, can be understood according to Halbwachs (1992) as part of a historical memory that informs and frames the way the past is conceived and experienced by different collectives and individuals residing in the region.

---

[36] This term is usually a synonym for Indigenous people but here the creoles also qualify as original inhabitants.

While the aborigines continue to be alterized by the dominant sectors of society for their preurban condition and their lack of integration, the creoles status as "original" inhabitants operates in a more ambiguous way. It is important to highlight that in the dominant and authorized narratives about Formosa's past, which have been pronounced by the local well-established traditional families and ratified by the local and provincial state, the urban whiteness first and foremost recognizes its origins in the military campaigns and in the arrival of European immigrants by train (Vardich, 2014). This locally constructed historical memory is based on and reproduces certain arguments present in the national historiography while simultaneously incorporating into these dominant versions of the past memories related to local non-Indigenous rural traditions. The latter is recognized as being a constitutive part of the region's folklore precisely because the creole elements represent for some residents the rural ancestry of their urban whiteness. In various cultural events and festivals that take place annually in urban contexts, the figure of the creole is celebrated as an icon of what is called "the traditional culture of western Formosa." Nevertheless, this act of folklorization in which creole and rural heritage is stressed does not imply that the residents in the urban space identify themselves as creoles. To summarize, in the official historical memory, the regional past is presented from an urban perspective, and in this construction based on the vision of the local elites, there is a greater degree of affinity and closeness between the identity demarcation categories "white town resident" and "rural creole" than between these two and the aborigines, no matter if the latter live in the urban or rural space.

In the narratives of the residents who do recognize a creole ancestry, none of whom belong to the town's elite, one can notice a type of elasticity between the categories "creole" and "white." In their accounts, once their families abandoned the rural space and ascended socially in an urban context, they stopped being "creole" and turned "white." This movement between identity categories expresses a process of whitening accompanied by mobility both in terms of class and space.

3.2.3 Indigeneity and the Political Dimension of Memory

When it comes to studying the collective memory of groups who have been historically marginalized and excluded from the dominant historical memories, not only are their alternative ways of building historicity to be taken into account but also the way memory can constitute for these groups a powerful tool in disputing senses of belonging and in the construction of political projects (Beckett, 1996). It is also important to take into account that official memories can be contested and challenged by memories produced by subordinated groups but these dominant narratives are also internalized to a certain degree by these very groups (Briones, 1994).

In this sense, categories such as "aborigine," which form part of the hegemonic social classification system, are internalized and reelaborated by the people who are ethnically demarcated in these terms. In the past decades, this subjectivation process has been affected by global and local revalorizations of Indigenous cultures and languages, nurtured by multicultural discourse and legal frameworks of recognition, making it possible for some Indigenous actors and activists to redeem being aborigine, leaving behind some of the historically constituted stigma.

In some parts of Argentina, Indigenous people emerged with force as political actors when their rights were incorporated into Argentina's National Constitution in 1994. However, in Formosa, this legal recognition began a decade earlier, in 1984, when the "Aboriginal Integral Law" was sanctioned, followed by the handing over of land titles to communities belonging to the four Indigenous people recognized as such in the province: Wichí, Western Toba, Pilagá and Eastern Toba (Spadafora et al., 2010). This didn't come out of thin air. In fact, already by the 1960s and 1970s, political capital was being mobilized in this region concerning the legal communitarian possession of land, driven by actors related to left-wing activism and organizations with a religious base who worked in an alliance with Indigenous community leaders (Leone, 2019, Spadafora et al., 2010). These mobilizations as well as the subsequent state policies of recognition should be understood in light of a growing Indigenous movement on a global scale but also in terms of local social and political dynamics (Leone Jouanny, 2015).

Regarding the Pilagá, a second process of political emergence was initiated between 2001 and 2003. The *Federación* was founded by various Pilagá leaders in an attempt to strengthen and unite their land claims and to construct autonomous Indigenous representation outside the provincial state agency, called "Institute of Aboriginal Communities," which was dedicated to develop and implement provincial and national policies related to Indigenous people.

Although the organization's agenda and dependency on external actors has varied over the years, in the past fifteen years, the leadership has dedicated a substantial amount of time and energy to monitoring and participating in a trial in which the Argentine state is accused of perpetuating a massacre against the Pilagá in October 1947. With a very brief history of organizational life, the *Federación* was invited by lawyers Carlos Díaz and Julio García to act as *Amicus Curiae*, without any binding participation, in the lawsuit these lawyers had filed in the Federal Court of Formosa in 2006. In the lawsuit charges were pressed against the state for having committed the massacre called "Rincón Bomba." These lawyers had made a draft of the events without the participation of the Pilagá, prioritizing written sources over the oral testimonies of the survivors (Salamanca, 2008, in Mapelman, 2015). Thus, for years, the Pilagá had no access to the written documentation presented in the lawsuit. To revert this situation, the *Federación* consulted with various human rights organizations and in 2014 gained access to the legal files. This also lead eventually to revoking the attorneys' legal authority in the lawsuit, designating the *Federación*'s own legal representative as their replacement, as well as turning some of the survivors of the massacre into the main claimants of the lawsuit (Mapelman, 2015). The court finally reached a verdict in 2019, ruling in favor of the claimants, recognizing the episode as a crime against humanity committed by the Argentine state.

When it comes to the *Federación*, their leaders have not only acquired technical knowledge through this judicial bureaucratic experience but have also built up and legitimized an agenda tied to the political dimension of memory. Nonetheless, the consolidation of the organization has been constantly challenged by legal and bureaucratic obstacles imposed by the provincial and national state agencies and their autonomy undermined by the pressures of the provincial party political machinery (Spadafora et al., 2010).

From a broader perspective, the trial concerning the massacre at Rincón Bomba has resulted both directly and indirectly in the mobilization of a subalternized collective memory that reveals the state's extermination acts, thereby confronting the dominant historical narratives in which the massacre is presented as an insignificant incident – a small-scale repression that saved the town of Las Lomitas from an assault on behalf of the local aggressive and insubordinate aborigines. The production of these contested memories has thus become a fertile ground for the second political emergence of the Pilagá, a process in which the *Federación* has had a central role.

3.3 Creole and Pilagá Film Reception

Here I present the findings from the fieldwork I carried out in Formosa, between 2013 and 2017, together with inhabitants who considered themselves descendants of the rural creoles cattle ranchers as well as with members of the Pilagá Indigenous people. Here I present and discuss screening and interview situations in which subjects belonging to each collective relate to the people and the places represented in the film. I also discuss how the screening activities are seen and how the film has been valued and used locally in each context.

3.3.1 Remembering a Rural Origin

In the case of the residents of the town of Las Lomitas who considered themselves descendants of the rural creoles cattle ranchers, most of the film screenings and interviews took place in their private homes together with their relatives, and only at times in more public spaces such as diners or offices. Attention was usually paid to the first third of the film, which introduces the members of the expedition, shows the hardships of their travel through the dense vegetation and presents the creole Calermo family.

Let's take a closer look at two of these screening events. The first one took place at Cacho[37] Calermo's home in 2014. A man in his late 70s, he was a well-known wire fence maker. He was a direct descendant of the Calermo family shown in the film. During the screening, he was accompanied by his partner Isolina (around sixty years old) and one of their daughters. The second screening I will refer to was organized in 2014 at Eusebia's place, where she runs both a simple diner and inn. Although Cacho, Isolina and Eusebia have different social standings in the present, they were all born and had grew up in the area that today extends between the *Bañado* and the border with Paraguay, where the Pilcomayo River passed up until the 1960s.

The film triggered stories about their origins and that of their families. This shared rural past was mostly valued positively and possible to redeem from an urban present. Isolina and Eusebia expressed affection for their rural origin, whereas Cacho claimed that he "barely remembered all that," expressing little interest and belonging to the place where he was born.

When an acquaintance entered her diner, Eusebia pointed at the black and white filmic images of eternal pastures and cried out: "this is my origin, I like my origin." Nonetheless, the materiality shown in the film didn't correspond entirely to what Eusebia remembered about her childhood. As we watched the Calermo family's ranch, Eusebia explained that her own family had never lived in such a simple house, theirs was "a house with a firm roof, . . . it was built with soil on top of which grass grew. I loved that. We had flowers on our roof." In other words, Eusebia didn't recognize her own rural past in the creole's material culture represented in the film. The memories of her mother's "round wooden cradle which was very pretty" contrasts with the crib in the movie, which she describes as "untidy" and "not very creole." Although she praised the Pilcomayo region as her rural origins, Eusebia distanced herself from what the images presented as typical of the creole settlers. She highlighted that her

---

[37] I have used pseudonyms in order to assure my interlocutors anonymity, except in the case of public figures or when their testimonies and texts have been published previously under their real names.

great-grandparents were Germans and that her father was a "great farmer" who didn't only work with cattle ranching but also grew pumpkins and other crops. In this sense, the elements of her family history that she stressed coincide with those valorized by the hegemonic narratives on the local past: the contribution of the European immigrants who arrived by train and the importance of sedentarized modes of production.

Unlike Eusebia, Isolina was thrilled to see the first scenes of the film and identified strongly with the filmed material world. Together with Cacho, she immediately recognized and commented on several artifacts used for horse riding and the rounding up of animals. These objects were described as being "from another time." Seeing the expeditioners moving forward on horseback, Isolina identified the saddle bag, explaining that it was used to carry the *mate*.[38] When I asked about its current use, her answer was ambiguous. We need to keep in mind that these memories about a rural past are activated from an urban present with few links to the countryside.

When watching the scenes that show the rounding up of livestock, Isolina referred to the men on horseback as "drovers." The images triggered memories of an artifact that is central to cattle ranching – the *corneta*[39] – an object that isn't visualized in the film. Encouraged by Isolina and their daughter, Cacho commented that he used to "ring the bell . . . going up front and calling the troop, I have forgotten all about that. I used to know how to ride horses." In order to round up the cattle troop, he remembered that he used a *corneta*, which was made from a bull's horn that sounded loud. The family discussed its characteristics, how it was manufactured and how it should be used. Isolina explained that the cow should not be called with the *corneta* from one's own home: "it isn't good to use it at home, it can bring betrayals and separations." This indicates the symbolic weight that this object carries in my interlocutors' memories. The positive appreciation of the *corneta* coincides with the way that this specific object is glorified and remembered with nostalgia in publications on western Formosa's folkloric tradition (García, 2014). In this sense, the creoles filmed by Hansson can be seen as representing those typical inhabitants of western Formosa who are redeemed by local experts in folkloric dancing and entertainment and marginally remembered in the dominant foundational narratives.

The images also triggered comments about what had caused the migration from the rural space to the urban one. Isolina commented how several families

---

[38] The container where the yerba mate is prepared and later drunk with a metal straw filter called a "bombilla." Mate is a popular hot tea-like drink consumed in large quantities in southern South America.

[39] A type of whistle that is used to call the cattle.

"suddenly got ready to leave" and moved to Las Lomitas. She explained that the people "grew poor" when they lost their cattle due to rabies: "we came because of the disease." For Isolina, the impoverishment and expulsion from the rural space was due to these circumstances and misfortunes. The migration from one space to another is remembered as something that happened suddenly.

Regarding the environment, the waters of the Pilcomayo River that continuously changed their course, producing flooding, have been recorded in the creole collective memory as a powerful historical agent. Referring to the formation of the *Bañado* in the 1970s, when the Pilcomayo River changed its course, Cacho explained that when the "*Bañado* arrived," they had to leave their place called El Descanso (most likely the location where the film was recorded), moving to another rural area. As for Eusebia, the images that came to mind when thinking about her childhood were those of when "the Pilcomayo changes," noting that it was "a great flood, similar to that of Noah's ark." She told me about one specific episode in which her whole family had to cross the river with supplies, cows and calves while it was flooding "when the *bañadero* was formed." Her father on horseback guided and supervised the transport of provisions from one shore to the other, while her mother "was swimming taking care of the calves," which were being carried on a raft. She remembered the "immense and flooding river of dark waters and endless turbulence." It is interesting to note that both Isolina and Eusebia attribute the changes their families underwent to environmental factors rather than human ones.

Isolina said that before migrating to the towns, they used to participate regularly in rural festivities. For various days, people would "eat, dance, listen to drums and violins, accordion, and the Virgin would be carried for miles, kilometers with the Virgin and the horses, others would be on foot with the music, something so fine. It was of another time." The festivities "were meant for dancing, not like today when the woman dances with her husband and no one else." Isolina appreciated the liberty of being able to dance with whoever. Thus, it became clear that the joy and liberty that reigned in the rural celebrations contrasted sharply with those organized in urban settings. Isolina regretted that there aren't any photographs depicting these festive occasions: "taking pictures would have permitted seeing what it was like." Although these celebrations are absent in the film, she identified with what the cinematographic narration shows since her own past is confirmed by those images.

Although Cacho confirmed that the man identified in the film as Anselmo Calermo was his grandfather (on his father's side), his comments on this topic were very brief. According to Isolina, Cacho's relationship with his father hadn't been very good. This might explain the silences around his father's genealogy. He didn't recognize his father amongst Anselmo's filmed children but he did identify his aunt Victoria who lived in Las Lomitas until her death. He identified her both by her name that the intertitle happened to announce and by her physical appearance.

Victoria is actually the only filmed subject who was visually recognized various times during the screening events and interviews that I have carried out with both audiences. In 2016, I met Cristina during a screening activity at one of the primary school located in the Pilagá community La Bomba, where she was a teacher. She told me with great enthusiasm that her great-grandmother Victoria, who she had had a close relationship with, appeared in the film. During my next visit, Cristina invited me to her house to see the film together with her father Juan, a retired military officer. While Cristina felt stimulated to learn more about her family history, Juan, who had been brought up by Victoria, wasn't sure he could recognize her in the film. Juan's reaction to the scenes in which the creole lifestyle was filmed was similar to that of Eusebia. Although he was born in the Pilcomayo region and was a direct descendant of the Calermos in the film, he was eager to mark a certain distance with what the film called creoles, exclaiming with a slight smile "they look so aborigine," pointing out their precarious living conditions. For Juan, it was the poverty the images revealed that made it possible to mistake the creole for aborigines. Here, we can see how the hegemonic stigmatizing association between indigeneity and poverty plays in Juan's interpretation of the film. This combined with his doubts about recognizing Victoria indicate that there is a certain resistance to accepting the filmic images as part of his own family history.

In these screening situations, my interlocutors expressed different degrees of identification with the creoles represented in the film. Juan and Eusebia who had become part of the town's property-owning middle class expressed distance with the creoles in the film, which they portrayed as poor, as a way of reasserting their current class belonging.

In general, my interlocutors expressed emotional memories that were based on what an individual remembers from his or her own life and the broader context in which it was spent. Only in a very few cases were more abstract images based on the memories of the older generation invoked. This indicated that the filmic images had operated as a "memory support," especially triggering memories related to the realm of actions and practices that a person had experienced during his or her life (da Silva Catela et al., 2010). Although individual memories are always framed and structured by collective and historical ones (Halbwachs, 1992), none of my interlocutors considered their emotional narratives of the past as representative of a larger group or collective. We also see how local dominant narratives dedicated to folklorizing the creole past have been internalized by some of my interlocutors, enabling the positive emotions triggered by the film.

With regards to my interlocutors' views on the act of screening an archive film and the value of the film itself, both Cacho and Eusebia were surprised that I had approached them and shown interest in their "origins" and family history. They weren't used to being interviewed by researchers, especially not by anthropologists. Eusebia thought I was from a TV station and dressed up for our first interview, assuming that there would be camera. As mentioned, in Formosa, anthropologists have almost exclusively studied Indigenous people, disregarding sectors of society that weren't ethnically demarcated. Since most of my interlocutors expressed a certain honor or pride of being interviewed, organizing screenings and interviews required fewer negotiations than when approaching the Pilagá.

Although my interlocutors were grateful that I had approached them with the film, none of them demanded that I give them a copy nor did they express any particular right over the material (for instance, as descendants of the represented creoles in film). When handing over a DVD with the film to Cacho, he asked me how much it would cost him. He was surprised to hear that I wanted him to have it for free, as a gift. After hearing about the film, Eusebia's daughter asked me if I could lend it to her for a couple of days. To them, the film couldn't be considered a gift (Mauss, 2009) but rather a commodity. The commercial value attributed to the film sheds light on how the screenings that I organized weren't necessarily seen by the audience that identified with it as an act of settling a debt. The film couldn't be considered a gift because there was no debt to be settled, no reciprocity to be followed up on. This deeply contrasted with the Pilagá situation, as will be seen later. From the creole point of view, the institutions or researchers didn't owe the people represented in their collections anything; and the film wasn't considered a type of heritage that could be claimed by proving cultural affiliation to the object.

3.3.2 Images of the Familiar Yet Foreign

I will now present a selection of screening situations, interviews and follow-up conversations with Pilagá interlocutors. I carried out screenings of the film both in private homes and in communal spaces.[40] Unlike the more public screenings that required negotiations with community leaders or school authorities, the screenings in family homes were carried out with greater flexibility and

---

[40] Most of my fieldwork was carried out in the Pilagá periurban communities La Bomba (located outside Las Lomitas) and Qompi (on the outskirts of Pozo del Tigre). I also visited the rural communities El Descanso, Cacique Coquero and Campo de Cielo.

spontaneity once a relationship of mutual trust had been established. The screenings generally summoned a solely Pilagá public, except for the school context, where teachers and authorities were "white." The Pilagá also paid close attention to the scenes that the intertitles attributed to their "own" ancestors.

I will describe three screenings that were carried out at my interlocutors' homes. First, my meeting with Pedro, survivor of the Rincón Bomba massacre, together with his son at his home in La Bomba; the second with Silvio and his relatives from El Descanso, carried out in a house on the outskirts of Las Lomitas that is used during their monthly visit to town; and finally the third with the retired leader José Rivero Zalazar at his home in Qompi. I will also include notes on the screening that was organized by one of the leaders of the *Federación* in 2013 as well as the discussions during a workshop on Indigenous history with José Rivero Zalazar and Ignacio Silva, an intercultural bilingual primary teacher, carried out in Qompi. All of my interlocutors, except for Pedro, were born after the 1947 Rincón Bomba massacre in the context of acute social and cultural transformations that affected the traditional Pilagá ways of life.

Many of my interlocutors commented during the screenings upon the endless grasslands (*pastizales* in Spanish) shown in the film, pointing out the absence of *monte*[41] in the past. It is well documented that, as the cattle ranching practice advanced from one province to the next looking for pasture for their livestock, these grasslands gradually disappeared and were replaced by *shrubland*, which appeared as a result of the rapid spread of seeds through the waste of the cattle (Gordillo, 2004). My interlocutors were well aware of this environmental transformation and used the word "*pastizales*" to refer to a temporality prior to that of the shrubland. This acute transformation was also presented as something hard to believe and imagine. Silvio, who was born in the 1950s, exclaimed when seeing the vast grasslands in the film that it was necessary "to [stop] believing that it is a lie when they [the elders] narrate," referring to how hard it was to believe the elders' oral descriptions of a landscape that had vanished. The film provided the visual evidence of this transformation while also confirming that the elders had not lied. Here, the materiality shown in the film coincided with the potent images transmitted by collective memory.

Both this particular type of landscape and the different *marisca*[42] techniques presented in the film were eagerly discussed. But there were other scenes in the film, related to dancing, singing and the consumption of tobacco and fermented beverages, that were more problematic to watch. These cultural practices and customs had been abandoned or deeply transformed as a result of the

---

[41] A type of shrubland that is hard to penetrate due to its dense vegetation.

[42] Local term for fishing, gathering and hunting.

sedentarization and evangelization process that took root after the 1947 massacre. In fact, the few reactions and comments about these scenes came from interlocutors who had witnessed or experienced them in their childhood or youth. In this sense, the interpretations of the film made by Pedro, born near the Pilcomayo River in the late 1930s, were central since he spoke of his own experiences of cultivating and consuming tobacco and participating in festivities and tribal dances before his religious conversion. When seeing some Pilagá smoking in the film, Pedro recalled: "I also had that seed [tobacco], I also planted it in El Descanso, I was a smoker." But immediately afterward, he condemned that habit, indicating that he quit when he entered the *evangelio*: "I don't know what our life is like, I left when I was 26 years old, I left all vices, I don't smoke or drink either." For Pedro, the images of the preparation of the *chañar* fruit, a tree commonly found in the Chaco region, triggered accounts about the brewing of the alcoholic beverage *aloja*,[43] relating it contemptuously to drunkenness rather than ritual use: "the elderly get drunk and then start singing." When watching the scene called the "great festive dance," both Pedro and Silvio described what they saw as the "toad dance" (*baile del sapo* in Spanish) or *nomí*.[44] They remembered participating in these dances when traveling to the neighboring province of Salta to work on the sugarcane plantations. Pedro explained with a grin on his face that at the end of each session, the woman would choose the man that she liked. The sexual liberty this type of dance entailed was negatively regarded by the Anglican and Franciscan missionaries (Citro, 2009, Gordillo, 2004) and would also be gradually banned by the Pentecostal *Iglesia Evangélica Unida*, which many Pilagá joined from the end of the 1940s.

As already mentioned, except for Pedro, the production and consumption of alcohol beverages made from fruits coming from the shrubland was seldom commented on. Instead, the images of the processing of *chañar* fruits, were associated with the healthy and tasty properties of the fruits and berries provided by the bush. Silvio spoke positively of the fruit of the carob tree (*algarroba* in Spanish), also common in the area, associating it with the good health of the "those from before." The interpretation offered by the intertitles was also challenged on this topic. The scene in which Pilagá women are chewing on *chañar* was interpreted by the Swedes as part of the elaboration of alcoholic

---

[43] Alcoholic beverage made from fruits and berries such as *mistol*, *algarroba* (carob tree) and *chañar*.

[44] These group dances were a type of seductive chain dance in which the men showed off their dancing skills to impress the women. Traditionally, they were danced during the festivities tied to the fruit harvest in the Chaco but later also common in the sugarcane factories in northwestern Argentina and other places to which Indigenous people from Chaco would migrate annually in search of work (Citro, 2009).

beverages. Silvio pointed out that the women weren't "spitting" in the bowls to kick-start fermentation, rather they were consuming the *chañar* by sucking out its nutrients, also known as *añapear*.

So far we have seen that in the reception of the film certain practices and material traces are praised while others are silenced or condemned. On the other hand, sadness and pity is also expressed. The lack of knowledge and possession of certain material goods such as clothes, chairs and bread are emphasized. When watching the naked women bathing, Pedro comments with a sigh that "the old ones went like that, without a shirt. Ohh. Before they didn't know of shirts." Not only were the "old ones" pitied for being poor since they possessed few commodities but also for not knowing the proper way to dress. This view of preevangelic Indigenous life is informed both by a religious morality that condemns nudity as well as by the hegemonic discourses that define the aborigines as poor. Simultaneously, this sadness also referred to direct experiences of suffering and hunger. When Pedro spoke of his own childhood, he exclaimed "how people suffered!" and asked me the rhetoric question: "Do you know what it is like to feel hunger?"

These readings and interpretations of what was paid attention to in the film indicate that my interlocutors felt a certain distance from the Pilagá portrayed in the film. The materiality and customs of those other Pilagá from the past were seen from the position of a new and regenerated ethnic identity strongly associated with their conversion to the *evangelio*. Although this conversion implied the juxtaposition of preevangelical and Christian values (Citro, 2009, Wright, 2008), the construction of a new Indigenous identity required a symbolic rupture with what was seen as representative of the traditional world of the "ancient ones" (*los antiguos* in Spanish). It is a paradox that although the Pilagá of today recognize that they are the direct descendants of the Pilagá in the movie, they are referred to as "people that no longer exist," as though it weren't only a question of ceasing to live but also implied the actual vanishing of a type of indigeneity. In this sense, the images were interpreted and felt familiar yet foreign.

I noticed that this ambiguous way of relating to the people and practices "from before" was one of the factors that conditioned the current political and social use of the film. In 2013, the Pilagá leader Noolé Cipriana Palomo organized a meeting in one of the communal spaces in Qompi, which included the screening of the film. The meeting took place in the context of negotiations for a national survey on Indigenous land tenure that state agencies were legally obliged to carry out as stated by law No. 26160. It had been sanctioned to attend to the countrywide Indigenous territorial emergency (Cardin, 2019). Around fifty people attended the meeting, including various authorities from nearby communities, teachers, women, youngster and children. After an informative talk about the law and its applicability, which was given by one of the *Federación*'s non-Indigenous advisers, and my own brief presentation of Hansson's film, Noolé asked the public before the screening began to pay attention to the territory, looking to "awaken memories about the ancestral territory." During this introduction, Noolé and the "adviser" emphasized that the filmed subjects had been "acting," thereby denying the documentary authenticity of the film and diverting the audience's attention away from the customs. It is worth mentioning that in a prior meeting with Noolé, we had discussed the conditions under which the film was shot, and I had told her that the documentary sources indicated that the Pilagá had been paid to act in the film.

To publicly highlight this "acting" can be understood as a way to challenge and deconstruct the "objectivity" and "realness" with which the ethnographic description of Pilagá life is presented in the film. It also offers a reading of intercultural relations based on the staging of Indigenous life. In conversations with other Pilagá interlocutors, putting on shows and staging traditional customs for a white public has been a recurring topic. From a perspective of a people that has been historically ethnographized, can acting and staging represent common modes of transmitting Indigenous traditions and practices to external actors?

So, while the filmed landscape was presented as a trace of a true "ancestral" territory, the scenes showing Indigenous customs were read as a fictionalization of native life, which in turn could be understood as a genuine way to communicate traditional customs to actors external to the community contexts.

During this event about reaffirming Indigenous rights, neither the Pilagá leader who organized the screening nor the public paid much attention to the Indigenous customs. I suggest that this scarcity of attention wasn't only due to a generalized difficulty to point out the current value of preevangelic practices, as seen earlier, but also informed by the specific way in which the Pilagá have emerged politically. This emergence was driven by a preoccupation and a sense of urgency in terms of land tenure, which had historically been articulated through sporadic collaborations between NGOs and Pilagá community leaders, as well as through the creation of the *Federación*. Unlike other Indigenous people in the region, whom in collaboration with NGOs had developed activities intended to recuperate traits of Indigenous traditional culture (Greco, 2016), the emphasis of the Pilagá had been on finding strategies to solve conflicts and make demands concerning Indigenous land tenure as well as generating evidence and arguments to prove that the massacre of Rincón Bomba actually had occurred.

A year after this event, Noolé insisted it was necessary to read the images in terms of Indigenous territory, this time stressing the "freedom" with which whole families could circulate in the past:

> To think that before they were free. The land was everything to them, they could move around, go back and forth. Because my mother told me . . . when it was the time of fruit abundance they were in one place, when it was fishing season they went to the banks of the river . . . The people were all with their families, the sister, the brother, the great grandfather . . . everyone went together to a place.

During the event, Noolé spoke of "ancestral territory," looking to strengthen and encourage land tenure demands. Here, she associated the territory represented in the film to a type of mobility based on seasonal circulation that was the basis of the Pilagá's social and economic organization prior to the conquest and colonization of their territories by foreign actors. In this sense, the film didn't only refer to a social order and time prior to the arrival of the "evangelio," in which there was an abundance of "vices" and poverty, but also stands for a time of territorial autonomy and a type of political and economic organization that changed drastically with the arrival of the white man.

As discussed, the film narrates the arrival of an expedition to the Pilagás' territory, making explicit the spatial coexistence of Europeans, creoles and Pilagá at the moment of the shooting. This narrative structure sparked memories and thoughts about the long process of submission and dispossession that the Pilagá have suffered. In a conversation with José Rivero Zalazar in 2014, he stressed his surprise at how the film presented the intertribal wars and the arrival of white man as contemporaneous events: "When you showed that movie I was surprised because I saw there was a white man together with the war that year, I didn't know that." Even though the expedition's diary suggests that the Pilagá had both traditional and new enemies simultaneously, in the memories, the interethnic wars were represented as pertaining to a temporality prior to the war against the white man. There was thus a type of discrepancy between the information provided by the film and Indigenous conceptions of historicity.

In other screening situations, although the images portrayed the relations between the Swedes, creoles and Pilagá as harmonious, they trigger accounts of violence perpetrated by Argentine military forces, and at times also by civilian creoles. This genealogy of state violence was especially emphasized in the workshop on Indigenous history that I organized in 2016 together with José Rivero Zalazar and Ignacio Silva. In the workshop, reflections on Pilagá history prevailed, although we also discussed briefly how the content of the film could be used by Indigenous teachers to transmit to their students information about their "culture," a notion used locally to refer to preevangelical rituals and festivities.

José and Ignacio spoke of the Indigenous people of Argentina in general terms, describing them as being victims of "dispersion." Then they spoke specifically of the Pilagá. "They were escaping from the massacre," says José, arguing that the current localization of Pilagá and Qom families in several provinces of Argentina had been the result of a long process of dispersion caused by various episodes of repression and state violence. This dispersion was commonly followed by obligatory sedentarization. José repeated various times that "before there were no fixed places," differentiating precolonial Indigenous mobility from the imposed "dispersion" and "sedentarization." Thus, "massacres," "dispersion" and "sedentarization," all caused by human actions and actors, became central topics that were used to explain the current demographic distribution of communities and families. In these narratives, there was a constant attempt to represent the past of a whole people, not just a few families or a personal life history. Although neither José nor Ignacio were at the time directly involved in the *Federación*, the recent mobilization of Pilagá memory about the Rincón Bomba massacre, in which critical views on the relations between Indigenous people and the Argentine state have been stressed, set the tone of the workshop. These readings resisted the filmic discourse that turned the Pilagá into exoticized objects of ethnographic observation and edutainment, isolating them from the broader context of submission and colonization of Indigenous lands and lives. In this sense, the interpretations anchored in a strong collective memory overflowed the filmic register and discourse opening up to readings against the grain. Constantly these more critical and political readings were intertwined with those that came from interpretation frameworks strongly informed by an evangelical present.

Unlike the creole reception, these screening situations revealed that Pilagá interlocutors rarely related what they viewed in the film with their own lived experience, since most of them were born or raised in a context of massive conversions to the *evangelio*. The recognition of the objects, actions and landscape represented in the film was mainly based on what had been told about the "old ones" or "ancient ones." In this sense, the film operated mainly as a "memory vehicle" (Jelin, 2002) that had the potential to awaken and activate collective memory about a temporality that hadn't been experienced by the viewer. The extensive and common references to what older generations had transmitted orally indicate that memory production is conceived by the actors as a collective endeavor and experience. Nonetheless, the authority of the elders' memories could also be questioned, their oral depictions considered "difficult to believe" and in need of being confirmed by visual evidence as such provided by the film.

With regards to the Pilagá's views on the act of presenting an archive film about them and the value of the film itself, as mentioned, the leadership of the *Federación* decided in a meeting in 2014 to support my research and screening activities in the communities. Various members of the organization emphasized the need to access and use this type of material, which could be used by the intercultural Pilagá teachers. This indicates that, according to the Pilagá authorities, the schools located in their communities would be one of the places where the film "belongs" and where it should be available and accessible. In this sense, the notion of a return "home," to the people represented in archives, commonly upheld in the literature on the subject, was confirmed by the opinions and views of the *Federación*'s leadership. Nonetheless, although I mentioned repeatedly the formal storage of the visual material in Sweden, no one questioned the legal possession of the images. It seems that the ease with which the film was digitally reproduced and multiplied in the field made it less relevant to pay attention to the institution that had been preserving it.

The *Federación* leadership also expressed their interest in pursuing and supporting research concerning the colonization process by which they were dispossessed of their land. As I spoke of the rich archive material on the encounter between the Swedes and the Pilagá, one of the leaders pointed out that it was important to speak in general terms about Pilagá history and to do research beyond concrete events such as the Rincón Bomba massacre, which had already been thoroughly studied.

Finally, it is also worth pointing out that during this meeting, just like in the workshop on Indigenous history, the film was considered a unique and useful source to show and teach the younger generations how ceremonies and festivities had been carried out in the past without having to invoke in the present the actual staging and performance of these practices. Actually, during my fieldwork, I observed only a very limited number of initiatives to revitalize and reenact what was locally known as "culture." In this specific case, the return of visual historical documents didn't become part of cultural revitalization processes, in which the practices represented in the archival sources were used as inspiration to reenact traditional ceremonies, because no such processes were in place at the time the return was carried out. As argued, this should be understood in terms of the specific political emergence of the Pilagá, anchored in territorial claims and in an interest in reconstructing colonization processes rather than revendicating their precolonial "culture."

Unlike the creoles, most of my Pilagá interlocutors knew exactly what an "anthropologist" was and had certain preconceived ideas about how I would go about doing my research. Many had been former informants to past generations of ethnographers. Some expected me to record what they said and reproached me when I didn't. In other cases, using a voice recorder was a problem, the explanation being that their words had already been "taken" from them. This idea of "extraction" was often accompanied by notions of "loss." I was told on one occasion that myths and tales of the "ancient ones" had been recorded for posteriority by people who didn't belong to their communities, who left and seldom came back. This gives us insight into the symbolic weight the act of returning ethnographic recordings of Pilagá "culture" can have in the present.

It is interesting to note that during my fieldwork in the communities, the Pilagá teachers, students, preachers and community leaders I spoke with commonly expected to receive as a gift not only a copy of the film but also paper prints of photographs taken by Hansson that portrayed the Pilagá. Although my intention was to hand them copies for free, just as I had with my creole interlocutors, sometimes more than I had planned to give was claimed or the demand was made before I had time to offer it. The representation of the Pilagá in the visual objects was what turned them into demandable gifts. Within a colonized logic of reciprocity, the film could be seen as something that was returned to the Pilagá to compensate for that which had been given by them or taken from them by external actors. Nonetheless, no return was big and important enough to symbolically make up for what had "left" them. For instance, once I asked Silvio which photograph he would like to have, and he answered that he wanted them all. The unlimited nature of the demands, as expressed by Silvio, represents the inability for the rest of society to give back or return what has historically been taken from the Pilagá or given by them to others. This is intimately related to the historical ethnographization and alterization of the Pilagá, in which anthropologists have had a central role.

3.3.3 Comparing Interpretations and Social Uses of a Returned Archive Film

Here I would like to review and discuss the main contrasts and similarities in the way the film has been interpreted and valued by both audiences and pay attention to nuances within each audience.

With regards to how memories are produced, there is stark difference between the two audiences. In fact, the way the film was approached depended both on generational belonging of the viewer as well as the way memory production was perceived and practiced by each audience. On one hand, the possibility of relating one's lived experience with that which is shown in the film depends in the case of both audiences on the age of the interlocutor as well as the temporal distance between the present and the moment during which each collective underwent deep historical transformations. Most Pilagá approached the film as a "vehicle of memory," since their understanding and comments of it were commonly based on what they had been told about that "other" temporality, prior to evangelization. However, Pedro, the eldest of my Pilagá interlocutors, narrated his own conversion to the *evangelio*, refering to his experience of the dancing, smoking and alcohol consumption presented in the film. When it comes to the residents with creole roots, the film was mostly approached as a "memory support" that helped them remember childhood memories of that "other" place from which they had been forced to migrate together with their families. Nonetheless, the younger generation, even though interested in the images, could only relate to them in terms of what they had been told. The fact that the migration of creole families to urban contexts occurred closer to the present than the evangelization of the Pilagá explains partially why in the creole reception the cattle ranching scenes were commonly compared to what the viewers had experienced in their childhood while the preevangelical Pilagá customs and practices were often interpreted through what had been said about "before."

Nonetheless, the film didn't only operate as a "vehicle of memory" for my Pilagá interlocutors due to this distance in time to the events that drastically changed their social and cultural configuration. Rather, this approach was privileged since it corresponded to a perception of memory production as something collective. This becomes clear when considering that in most occasions the film sparked narratives on the destiny and fate of an entire people, referring constantly to the words of the elders. During the creole reception, the film triggered reflections and memories referred to in individual biographies or family histories, which were at no point perceived as constituted collectively. This stark difference in how memory is understood and practiced by each audience also defines the way the film is approached.

Even though my interlocutors with creole roots didn't perceive their own memory practices as framed by a collective memory, they did speak of the historical transformations their families had suffered, attributing the causes of the migration from the rural space to environmental factors, such as the changing course of the Pilcomayo and the coming of diseases. Their historical interactions with Indigenous people in the rural space and their role in settling in an Argentine border region weren't topics of major concern. With regards to the Pilagá's attempt to understand the historical transformations that they have undergone, human intentional and organized actions were commonly identified as the main agents of change. Although the reasons for their evangelization process wasn't a common topic of discussion, their forced sedentarization was profusely commented upon. Dispersion and sedentarization were presented as elements of a historical process that was violently forced upon them. In the workshop as well as in the activities carried out by the *Federación*, I observed a shared agenda of confronting the regional dominant narratives that, albeit the recognition of Indigenous rights, kept on characterizing the aborigines as poor and in need of assimilation. In the case of the creole descendants, I have noted no such contested versions of the past. The overall nostalgic and emotional tone and the comments on the materiality related to cattle ranching and rural life reproduced the folkloric aspect of creoleness, which had been legitimized in the local hegemonic discourses.

The historical transformations that were dramatically and emotionally depicted by both audiences during the screenings have also marked the current identity ascriptions of each collective as well as the way each of them experience the past. Just as has been argued in the case of other evangelized and colonized Indigenous people in the Chaco (Citro, 2009, Wright, 2008), the Pilagá's conversion to the *evangelio* together with the stigmatization produced by hegemonic discourses have deeply affected their visions of the past and the way they relate to those "ancient ones" who lived in precolonial times. Primarily, the identity position as "new" and "converted" implies a temporal break, separating the "time of the new" from the "time of before." Nonetheless, this relation to a "prohibited" and "stigmatized" past is currently complemented by the mobilization of memories that confront dominant historical narratives, making it also possible to conceive of the past as a time of freedom and autonomy that was interrupted by massacres and other types of violence suffered by the Pilagá.

In the case of the creole descendants, their current understanding of the past is used to reinforce their urban "white" identity. Unlike the Pilagá, this doesn't require a temporal break with their past but rather a symbolic and experiential dislocation from the rural space as well as a silencing of their role in the colonization and appropriation of Indigenous land, in line with the local historical hegemonic memory. Hence, I argue that the descendants of the creoles see their "own" identity and past in the film, based on a temporal continuity and a spatial discontinuity marked by the passage from the rural to the urban space, while the Pilagá express a more abrupt temporal discontinuity and a relative spatial continuity, given their evangelical experience of a new and regenerated identity and their enduring inhabitation of rural areas.

With regards to the potential social and political uses of the film in the present, the authorities of the *Federación* have expressed the value of the film in educational contexts and on one occasion it was used in a meeting to activate and reaffirm the memories about their ancestral and traditional lands. It is interesting to note that although the film can be used to teach the younger generations about their "culture," its content doesn't provide the clues and evidence needed in the current research agenda on massacres and other injustices suffered by the Pilagá in the past. Nonetheless, due to the Pilagá's generalized perception of temporal discontinuity and to the specific characteristics of their political emergence, the religious and ceremonial preevangelical practices shown in the film haven't been reinvindicated politically to strengthen and revitalize their sense of indigeneity. During the past two decades, the *Federación* has recognized and validated the potential of collective memory to correct official history writing, to reassert their rights as Indigenous people and to obtain reparations for historical injustices. Instead of valorizing, reactivating and reenacting precolonial practices, their political emergence has mobilized memories that have enabled and encouraged testimonies and reflections upon the colonizing process and the historical transformations suffered by the Pilagá. In addition, this mobilization of subalternized memories has implied both recognizing the political and social dimension of memory as well as its potential to be activated and mobilized through "memory work" (Jelin, 2002).

Unlike the Pilagá, the creole descendants weren't organized politically and socially as a consolidated group but rather identified themselves as residents of the town where they were living. This might be a key factor in explaining their limited political and social use of the film. During the screenings, the film was used as type of family picture album, even by the viewers who didn't identify their relatives in the film. It was a way to access and activate their personal childhood experience from different social class positions in the present.

The potential social and political use of the film is intimately linked to the value attributed to it and how the screenings that I have organized have been seen by each audience. While many of my Pilagá interlocutors expected me to give them copies of what I was presenting to them, as demandable gifts, the residents with creole roots, who also recognized their past in the film, treated the material as a commodity. The projection of a commercial value upon the film indicates that the screenings weren't seen by the creoles as an act of historical reparation but rather as a simple act of letting them know of the existence of a commodity that could be of interest to them since it concerned their family history. As seen, although marginalized in Formosa society and historically expulsed from the rural space, the creoles hadn't been ethnically demarcated historically nor did they constitute in the present subjects with the right to claim for historical reparation, as is the case with Indigenous people. This made it possible to claim the past shown in the images as their own without claiming the right to have them returned to them.

The constant demands of digital or material copies made by various Pilagá interlocutors as well as the *Federación*'s interest in turning the film into pedagogical material to be used by the schools located in the Indigenous communities not only reveals a position that stresses the ethical rights of subjects represented in archival material over their images but also indicates how important it is to guarantee a collective accessing of the material through its storage and use in school contexts.

These stark contrasts in how projects of digital return are understood and received in the field heavily depend on the degree to which the audiences have been historically ethnographized and alterized and the way they are politically emerging in the present.

4 Final Reflections: Reframing Ethnographic Heritage

In this final section, I discuss how my combined archival and field approach and the results of my research can contribute to the current debate on the historical and contemporary relations between heritage institutions and the people represented in their collections. I also want to highlight through the cases I have studied some new topics and questions that can help orient future projects and research on "ethnographic returns."

A number of scholars in the field of heritage studies have pointed out how focusing too much on institutional, authorized and official heritage processes can limit our understanding of the complex relations developed between heritage-holding institutions and extrainstitutional stakeholders and actors (Crespo, 2017, Harrison, 2010). By carrying out extensive fieldwork, I stress the importance of obtaining in-depth understandings of extrainstitutional paradigms of value and repertoires of practice and meaning production that can be contrasted with authorized heritage discourses and practices.

As a starting point, I have resisted conceiving of heritage as something given, preferring to see it as something that exists thanks to the skein of politics and poetics that constitutes it (Crespo, 2017). This is why I dedicate the first section of the Element to the documentation and analysis of the complex process by which filmic images, produced under logics of edutainment, eventually acquired heritage status as ethnographic visual documentation, guaranteeing its conservation within an institution until today. By adopting a cultural biographical approach, it was possible to trace uses and values given to an archive film throughout its life, reconstructing the process by which it was turned into heritage. I stress that the act of returning material labeled as "ethnographic" to the sites from which it was historically extracted requires one to acknowledge the authorized status of the material being returned.

Nonetheless, the archival work didn't only give me insight into the process by which the filmic material became heritage. By approaching the documents generated by the travelers as both authorized discourse as well as historical sources, it was possible to reconstruct the social situation in which the film was shot. Reading the expedition's diary in dialogue with current historical and anthropological research on the region was a way of endowing my ethnographic fieldwork with temporal depth. In this sense, the combination of archival techniques with an ethnographic field approach proved to be methodologically productive when studying the return of archive images. On one hand, it contributed to understanding the historical transformations between the moment of capture and the moment of return. Also, the historical perspective gave me clues to understand the historical process that had led to the present while the memories triggered by the film gave me deeper insight into how the same historical process was experienced by people demarcated as non-Indigenous and Indigenous.

Furthermore, understanding the historical moment of capture as well as that of return in their own terms can be a way to avoid projecting the social categories that appear in the archives upon the contemporary social reality and vice versa. These categories, which operate as social limits, change over time, making it a task in itself to identify and locate in the present the communities, groups or individuals who see their own past in the visual or physical collections being returned. As seen in this Element, even if the digital access to copies of the images is claimed, the way of life represented in the film may not be entirely revindicated. Nor does the identification with the filmed past guarantee that the material will be claimed based on the ethical right of the represented.

When analyzing actions of return, I have shown that their reception is characterized by the production of memories as well as affect. The film was not only watched but also experienced affectively, socially constituted and structured by emotional meaning systems (Lutz and White, 1986). My interlocutors expressed emotions when recognizing objects, landscapes or people in the film but also when the film triggered memories of events, places and practices that were absent in the film. Unlike the scientific authority and distance with which heritage institutions handle and understand the materials that they conserve, their memorial and affective dimension is stressed when apprehended by noninstitutional paradigms of value and practice. I also stress that the affective dimension of the return didn't undermine the knowledge and authority with which my interlocutors spoke of the images. Unlike the version of the past offered by the film, which was authorized by the archive, my interlocutors' own authority stemmed from what the elders or their relatives had told them and in some cases from their own memories and experience of what the film showed and narrated. It was this type of affective and memorial knowledge that made it possible to confirm, doubt or question what the film presented as an objective document of both groups' tangible and intangible heritage. In this sense, during my fieldwork, I observed both encounters and/or disagreements between the filmic narrative authorized by the archive and the readings anchored in an affective and memorial reception of the images.

This has led me to consider the relations between memory production and images. One could describe the screening events as moments in which the material filmic image and narrative is confronted or confirmed with the immaterial images the viewer carries about his or her own past. Encounters or confrontations between what Belting (2007) calls internal and external images. According to this author, external images are created and preserved through a material medium while internal images are processed by the human perception, both being constitutive one of the other. The film has thus been interpreted and read through internal images that represent lived experience as well as transmitted perceptions of what has been experienced by past generations. These internal immaterial images with which the film is viewed are expressed by individuals who belong to differentiated social groups, thus representing different collective memories (Halbwachs, 1992) and modes of memory production and transmission. These interpretations and the way the material print of the past was experienced and felt were also conditioned by each group's specific historical experience and their present identity ascriptions, as well as the way each collective had been affected by the hegemonic formation of alterity. But at the same time, this diversity is limited and conditioned by the uniformity of a historical memory that is imposed as historical truth through history writing and the transmission of a selection of historical events and heroes to a nationally or regionally defined citizenship (Briones, 1994). Thus, it can be considered that while the film is but a set of moments that have been captured and fixed materially by travelers, the internal images about the same region and its people are nurtured by the accumulation of lived experience as well as what has been transmitted by memory from one generation to the other conditioned by the hegemonic narratives of the past.

Regarding these encounters and confrontations between the material filmic image and narrative and immaterial images, I noted that it was more common to doubt or question the textual interpretations expressed through the intertitles than the visuality of the filmed scenes. Apart from one occasion, in which the acting of the filmed subjects was emphasized, the scenes were commonly understood in a realistic manner, as visual evidence that could validate the viewers' life experience or what the elders had transmitted about the past. But, unlike the filmed scenes, the explanations offered by the intertitles were doubted or directly corrected, challenging aspects of the authorized heritage discourse present in the script. Attention was also drawn to details that could be visualized in the images but weren't commented upon in the intertitles.

It is interesting to note that the social conformation of the region, as represented in the film script, coincided almost identically with the present hegemonic categories of demarcation and self-demarcation in Formosa. According to the film, the Chaco was socially constituted by creoles and Pilagá but it also represented visually the travelers own arrival to the region. Although the expedition members didn't refer to themselves as "white" in the script, during the return it became clear that the prevailing hegemonic social classification, in which whites and creoles were distinguished from aborigines, was projected upon the three groups visualized in the film, associating the travelers with the "whites" who settled the region.

Nonetheless, although the story told by the film narrative and material images was confirmed in terms of social composition, it didn't necessarily coincide with the potent images transmitted by memory processes. The filmic images commonly triggered accounts of events, people and objects that weren't represented in the film. Only in the case of the Pilagá did these memories implicitly contradict the story told by the script. While the narrative structure of the film presented the relations between whites, creoles and Pilagá as friendly, emphasizing the wars and conflicts between Indigenous groups, José, Ignacio and Noolé spoke extensively about the conquest of Indigenous territories and the violence with which they had been massacred, dispersed and forcefully sedentarized, not by other Indigenous people but by non-Indigenous actors. These readings of what was absent in the film coincided with the violent social situation under which the shots were taken, as recorded in the expedition's diary. Nonetheless, these insights into Indigenous history weren't used by my interlocutors to unauthorize the film. Rather, the way the film's edition narrated the expedition's encounter with the Pilagá, under threat of the Nivaklé, was read by José as proving the contemporaneity of the intertribal wars and the war with the white man. In this sense, the film was seen as a document or source that contributed to a better understanding of Indigenous history.

Even though there were often disagreements between the authorized filmic narrative and the way the past was remembered through memory practice,

I argue that the realism and the hegemonic social categories with which the film was interpreted made it difficult to decenter and destabilize its narrative. Although the intertitles might have been considered as representing outsider perspectives that could be scrutinized, the visuality of the film wasn't questionable, understood as evidence and documentation of a past reality. Furthermore, the weight of the hegemonic categories of whiteness, creoleness and indigeneity in the shared present interpretative frameworks contributed to naturalize instead of question the filmic representations of colonizing explorers and settlers and of the Pilagá as a vanishing people. So, although I have produced situations in which the archive film was opened up to interpretative regimes tied to the affective and memorial dimension of what was represented, the readings that were generated outside the context of the archive were still marked by what the hegemonic situation permitted.

Not only did my research reveal that little energy was invested in confronting and contesting what the film defined as Pilagá and creole cultural heritage, but fundamentally I discovered how it was necessary to decenter the Western institutional concept of heritage (Winter, 2013) to understand how the act of return was conceived locally. As seen, there was a stark contrast between how both audiences regarded where the film "belonged" and the way it ought to circulate and be accessed. Unlike the descendants of the creoles who treated the film as a mere commodity that could illuminate their family history, the Pilagá asserted their right to be given a copy of the film and were concerned about how the film could be accessed by teachers and students. Although the Pilagá didn't recognize visually any individual, they embraced every filmed Pilagá as a common ancestor, representing the preevangelical "ancient ones." By claiming a digital copy of the material, their rights as descendants of the filmed subjects were emphasized. This way of relating to the archive film, as something that belonged and was owed to the Pilagá as a people, made it possible to consider its current circulation in the communities as a result of a return "home" where it belongs.

Although critical approaches to heritage studies have identified and contrasted official and nonofficial heritage practices (Harrison, 2010), by studying in depth the audiences' interpretative framework and the categories with which they engage in memory practices, it was possible to identify valorizations and uses of the past that don't necessarily constitute heritage practices, in the sense of an impulse of conservation from below (Samuel, 1994). I argue that it is necessary to consider a diversity of impulses coming from below. In the case of the Pilagá, the emphasis on collective access, free circulation and digital reproduction offers alternative views on how archival material should be handled. Here the accessibility and active use of archival material is prioritized over its formal possession and permanent store. In addition, stressing the role of Indigenous teachers in handling and transmitting the content of the film to their students also makes it necessary to consider how returned "ethnographic" data isn't only read in terms of what it can reveal about the past but also in terms of what it can mean and represent for future generations.

References

Abduca, R., Escolar, D., Villagrán, A., & Faberman, J. (2014) Debate: "Historia, antropología y folklore." Reflexiones de los autores y consideraciones finales de la editora. *Corpus. Archivos virtuales de la alteridad americana*, **4**, 1–23.

Andermann, J., & Simine, S. (2012) Introduction: Memory, Community and the New Museum. *Theory Culture & Society*, **29**(1), 3–13.

Arce Bazán, F. (2013) *El Doctor del Pueblo*. Formosa: Mega Imagen.

Arenas, P. (2011) Ahora Damiana es Krygi. Restitución de restos a la comunidad aché de Ypetimi. Paraguay. *Corpus*, **1**(1).

Beck, H. (2007) La vida en las fronteras interiores del territorio formoseño. La naturaleza hostil del último baluarte aborigen. *XI Jornadas Interescuelas/ Departamentos de Historia*, San Miguel de Tucumán: Facultad de Filosofía y Letras. Universidad de Tucumán.

Beck, H. (2010) La política oficial contra los derechos de los pobladores en áreas del bañado La Estrella de Formosa. Historia de un conflicto. In O. Mari, G. Mateo & C. Valenzuela (Eds.), *Territorio, poder e identidad en el agro argentino*. Buenos Aires: Imago Mundi, pp. 61–84.

Beckett, J. (1996) Against Nostalgia: Place and Memory in Myles Lalor's "Oral History." *Oceania*, **66**(4), 312–327.

Bell, J. (2003) Looking to See: Reflections on Visual Repatriation in the Purari Delta, Gulf Province, Papua New Guinea. In L. Peers & A. Brown (Eds.), *Museums and Source Communities*. London & New York: Routledge, pp. 111–122.

Bell, J., Christen, K., & Turin, M. (2013) Introduction: After the Return. *Museum Anthropology Review*, **7**(1–2), 1–21.

Belting, H. (2007) *Antropología de la imagen*. Buenos Aires, Katz editores.

Benjamin, Walter (2008 [1940]) *Tesis sobre la historia y otros fragmentos*. Mexico City: Ítaca.

Boast, R., & Enote, J. (2013) Virtual Repatriation: It's Neither Virtual nor Repatriation. In P. Biehl & C. Prescott (Eds.), *Heritage in the Context of Globalization: Europe and the Americas*. New York: Springer, pp. 103–113.

Bossert, F., & Siffredi, A. (2011) Las relaciones interétnicas en el Pilcomayo medio: la guerra indígena y sus transformaciones (1882–1938). *Población & Sociedad*, **18**, 3–48.

Briones, C. (1994) Con la tradición de todas las generaciones pasadas gravitando sobre la mente de los vivos: usos del pasado e invención de la tradición. *RUNA archivo para las ciencias del hombre*, **21**, 99–129.

Briones, C. (2002) Mestizaje y blanqueamiento como coordenadas de aboriginalidad y nación en Argentina. *RUNA*, **23**, 61–88.

Briones, C. (2004) Construcciones de aboriginalidad en Argentina. *Journal de la Société Suisse des Americanistes*, **68**, 73–90.

Briones, C. (2005) Formaciones de alteridad: contextos globales, procesos nacionales y provinciales. In C. Briones (Ed.), *Cartografías argentinas*. Buenos Aires: Antropofagia, pp. 11–43.

Buckley, L. (2014) Photography and Photo-elicitation after Colonialism. *Cultural Anthropology*, **29**, 720–743.

Cardin, L. (2019) Relevamiento territorial de los Pueblos Indígenas. Riesgos y desafíos. *Papeles de Trabajo*, **13**(23), 30–49.

Christen, K. (2011) Opening Archives: Respectful Repatriation. *The American Archivist*, **74**, 185–210.

Citro, S. (2009) *Cuerpos significantes: Travesías de una etnografia dialéctica*, Buenos Aires: Biblos.

Collier, J. (1957) Photography in Anthropology: A Report on Two Experiments. *American Anthropologist*, **59**, 843–859.

Coquero, O. (1999) Historia de las comunidades: Cacique Coquero. In A. Vidal (Ed.), *Narrativa y Conflicto*. Formosa: CECAZO, INAI.

Cordeu, E., & Siffredi, A. (1971) *De la algarroba al algodón. Movimiento Mesiánico de los guaycurú*, Buenos Aires: Juarez Editor.

Crespo, C. (2017) Processes of Heritagization of Indigenous Cultural Manifestations: Lines of Debate, Analytical Axes and Methodological Approaches. In O. Kaltmeier & M. Rufer (Eds.), *Entangled Heritages: (Post-)colonial Perspectives on the Uses of the Past in Latin America*. London & Paris: Routledge, pp.153–174.

Cuarterolo, A. (2011) El viaje en la era de la reproductibilidad técnica. Discursos etnogeográficos en los primeros travelogues argentinos. In M. Giordano & A. Reyero (Eds.), *Identidades en foco. Fotografía e investigación social*. Resistencia: IIGHI-CONICET/FADyCC-UNNE.

da Silva Catela, L., Giordano, M., & Jelin, E. (2010) Introducción. In L. Da Silva Catela, M. Giordano & E. Jelin (Eds.), *Fotografía e identidad. Captura por la cámara, devolución por la memoria*. Buenos Aires: Trilce.

Dell Arciprete, A. (1991) Lugares de los pilagá. *Hacia una nueva carta étnica del Chaco*, **II**, 58–85.

Edwards, E. (2003) Talking Visual Histories: Introduction. In L. Peers & A. Brown (Eds.) *Museums and Source Communities*. London & New York: Routledge, pp. 83–99.

Fernández Bravo, A. (2013) El etnógrafo como contrabandista. Tráfico de imágenes, propagación de conceptos y usos de la cultura material en la obra de Alfred Métraux. *Cuadernos de literatura*, **17**(33), 224–252.

Fuhrmann, W. (2013) Ethnographic Film Practices in Silent German Cinema. In J. Bell, A. Brown & R. Gordon (Eds.), *Recreating First Contact: Expeditions, Anthropology, and Popular Culture*. Washington, DC: Smithsonian Institution, pp. 41–54.

Furhammar, L. (1991) *Filmen i Sverige*, Stockholm: Förlags AB Wiken.

García, B. (2014) *El criollo del Oeste, su historia, su cultura*. Formosa: Ministry of Culture and Education.

García Canclini, N. (1993) Los usos sociales del patrimonio cultural. In E. Florescano (Ed.), *El Patrimonio Cultural de México*. Mexico City: F.C.E.

Gaudreault, A. (1987) Narration and Monstration in the Cinema. *Journal of Film and Video*, **39**, 29–36.

Giordano, M. (2010) Las comunidades indígenas del Chaco frente a los acervos fotográficos de "sus" antepasados. Experiencias de (re)encuentro. In L. Catela, M. Giordano & E. Jelin (Eds.), *Fotografía e identidad. Captura por la cámara, devolución por la memoria*. Buenos Aires: Trilce, pp. 21–58

Giordano, M. (2018) Experiencias de viaje y exotización en expediciones al Gran Chaco (1900–1930). In M. Giordano (Ed.), *De lo visual a lo afectivo. Prácticas artísticas y científicas en torno a visualidades, desplazamientos y artefactos*. Buenos Aires: Biblos, pp. 199–225.

Gordillo, G. (2001) Un río tan salvaje e indómito como el indio toba: una historia antropológica de la frontera del Pilcomayo. *Desarrollo Económico*, **41**, 261–280.

Gordillo, G. (2004) *Landscapes of Devils: Tensions of Place and Memory in the Argentinean Chaco*. Durham, NC, & London: Duke University Press.

Gordillo, G., & Hirsch, S. (2003) Indigenous Struggles and Contested Identities in Argentina Histories of Invisibilization and Reemergence. *Journal of Latin American Anthropology*, **8**, 4–30.

Greco, L. (2016) "Mi cultura la tengo, pero no la practico." Reflexiones sobre las movilizaciones de la cultura y los pueblos indígenas en Ingeniero Juárez, Formosa, Argentina. *Etnografías Contemporáneas*, **2**, 176–203.

Griffiths, A. (1999) "To the World the World We Show": Early Travelogues as Filmed Ethnography. *Film History* **11**, 282–307.

Grimshaw, A. (2001) *The Ethnographer's Eye. Ways of seeing in Anthropology*. Cambridge: Cambridge University Press.

Gustafson Reinius, L. (2015) I återskenet av utbrunnen eld. Om delandet av fotografiska samlingar. In M. Larsson, A. Palmskiöld, H. Hörnfeldt &

L. Jönsson (Eds.), *I utkanter och marginaler. 31 texter om kulturhistoria.* Stockholm: Nordiska Museets förlag.

Gustavsson, A. (2016) Prácticas de exploración y colonización. Relatos de Mauricio Jesperson sobre el Gran Chaco durante la primera mitad del siglo XX. *Folia Histórica*, **27**, 39–62.

Gustavsson, A. (2018a) Imagen fílmica, praxis expedicionaria y colonización: historias y memorias de los pilagá y criollos del Chaco argentino. Doctoral dissertation Institute for High Social Studies at the National University of General San Martín, Argentina.

Gustavsson, A. (2018b) Praxis expedicionaria y tecnología fílmica en la frontera del Pilcomayo en 1920. In M. Giordano (Ed.), *De lo visual a lo afectivo. Prácticas artísticas y científicas en torno a visualidades, desplazamientos y artefactos.* Buenos Aires: Biblos, pp. 257–278.

Gustavsson, A., & Giordano, M. (2013) The Pilagá of the Argentine Chaco through an Exoticizing and Ethnographic Lens: The Swedish Documentary Film Following Indian trails by the Pilcomayo River. *Journal of Aesthetics and Culture*, **5**(1), 21562.

Halbwachs, M. (1992) *On Collective Memory.* Chicago: Chicago University Press.

Halperín Donghi, T. (1982) *Una nación para el desierto argentino*, Buenos Aires: Centro Editor de América Latina.

Hansson, W. (1943) Haegers Expedition. In C. Munthe (Ed.), *Chacofarare Berätta.* Gothenburg: Hugo Gerbers Förlag.

Harrison, R. (2010) Heritage as Social Action. In S. West (Ed.), *Understanding Heritage in Practice.* Manchester: Manchester University Press and Open University, pp. 240–276.

Hedling, E., & Jönsson, M. (2007) *Välfärdsbilder: svensk film utanför biografen. Amatörfil, beställningsfilm, undervisiningsfilm speglar 1900talets välfärdssamhälle*, Stockholm: Carlssons.

Henley, P. (2020) *Beyond Observation: A History of Authorship in Ethnographic Film.* Manchester: Manchester University Press.

Hennessy, K. (2009) Virtual Repatriation and Digital Cultural Heritage: The Ethics of Managing Online Collections. *Anthropology News*, **50**(4), 5–6.

Hennessy, K. (2016) From the Smithsonian's MacFarlane Collection to Inuvialuit Living History. In S. Chiel van den Akker (Ed.), *Museums in a Digital Culture.* Amsterdam: Amsterdam University Press.

Henry, J., & Henry, Z. (1944) *Doll Play of Pilagá Indian Children*, New York: Orthopsychiatric Association.

Hutton, P. H. (1993) *History as an Art of Memory.* Hannover & London: University Press of New England.

Idoyaga Molina, A. (1996) Entre el mito y la historia. La mitificación de un líder mesiánico. *Scripta Ethnológica*, **18**, 167–183.

Jelin, E. (2002) *Los trabajos de la memoria*, Madrid & Buenos Aires: Siglo XXI.

Jernudd, Å. (1999) *Oscar Olsson's African Films. Examples of Touristic Edutainment*. Örebro:Örebro University.

Jesperson, M. (1941) *En Lundensare i Chaco*. Stockholm, Norstedt.

Jesperson, M. (1942) *En Svensk Caballero vid Pilcomayo*. Stockholm, Norstedt.

Jesperson, M. (1943a) *I Vildmarkens vald*. Stockholm, Folket i Bilds Förlag.

Jesperson, M. (1943b) Indianliv. In C. Munthe (ed.), *Chacofarare berätta*. Stockholm, Hugo Gebers Förlag, pp. 89–119

Karsten, R. (1932) *Indian Tribes of the Argentine and Bolivian Chaco*. Helsingfors: Societas Scientiarum Fennica.

Kopytoff, I. (1986) The Cultural Biography of Things: Commoditization as Process. In A. Appadurai (Ed.), *The Social Life of Things: Commodities in Cultural Perspective*. Cambridge: Cambridge University Press, pp. 70–73.

Lazzari, A. (2003) Aboriginal Recognition, Freedom and Phantoms: The Vanishing of the Ranquel and the Return of the Rankülche in La Pampa. *Journal of Latin American Anthropology*, **8**, 59–83.

Lazzari, A. (2008) La restitución de los restos de Mariano Rosas: identificación fetichista en torno a la política de reconocimiento de los ranqueles. *Estudios de Antropología Social*, **1**(1), 35–64.

Lenton, D. (1997) Los Indígenas y el Congreso de la Nación Argentina: 1880–1976. *Revista Naya*, **2**.

Lenton, D. (2010) Política indigenista argentina: *una construcción inconclusa Anuário Antropológico*, **1**, 57–97.

Leone Jouanny, M. (2015) Entre reordenamiento de tierras y reivindicaciones históricas. El proceso de conformación de la Ley Integral del Aborigen en Formosa. *Trabajo y Sociedad*, **25**, 265–280.

Leone, M. (2019) "Por la liberación del indígena." Trabajo pastoral y procesos de organización política indígena en la región del Chaco argentino (1965–1984). *Sociedad y Religión*, **29**, 112–141

Lois, C. (2001) Desierto y territorio: imágenes decimónicas del Gran Chaco argentino. *Mundo de Antes*, **2**, 97–116.

Lutz, C., & White, G. M. (1986) The Anthropology of Emotions. *Annual Review of Anthropology* **15**(1), 405–436.

Maeder, E., & Gutiérrez, R. (1995) *Atlas Histórico del Nordeste Argentino*, Resistencia: IIGHI-UNNE.

Mapelman, V. (2015) *Octubre Pilagá. Memorias y archivos de la masacre de La Bomba*, Buenos Aires: Tren en Movimiento.

Mason, P. (2001) *The Lives of Images*. London: Reaktion.

Mauss, M. (2009) *Ensayo sobre el don. Forma y función del intercambio en las sociedades arcaicas*, Buenos Aires: Katz.

Métraux, A. (1937) Études d'Ethnographie Toba-Pilagá (Gran Chaco). *Anthropos*, **32**, 171–194, 378–401.

Métraux, A. (1946a) *Myths of the Toba and Pilagá Indians of the Gran Chaco. Memoirs of the American folklore Society*, **40**, 1–179.

Métraux, A. (1946b) Indians of the Gran Chaco. Ethnography of the Chaco. In J. Steward (Ed.), Volume I of *Handbook of South American Indians*. Estados Unidos: Smithsonian Institute.

Miller, E. (1979) *Los toba argentinos. Armonía y Disonancia en una sociedad*, Mexico City: Siglo XXI.

Mitchell, W. (2003) Mostrando el ver. Una crítica de la cultura visual. *Estudios Visuales: Ensayo, teoría y critica de la cultura visual y el arte contempóraneo*, **1**, 17–40.

Newbery, S. (1983) Vigencia de los mitos de origen en la cosmovisión pilagá y toba. *Cuadernos del INAPL*, **10**, 123–140.

Nilsson Stutz, L. (2013) Claims to the Past. A Critical View of the Arguments Driving Repatriation of Cultural Heritage and Their Role in Contemporary Identity Politics. *Journal of Intervention and State Building*, **7**(2), 170–195.

O'Neal, J. (2013) Going Home: The Digital Return of Films at the National Museum of the American Indian. *Museum Anthropology Review*, **7**(1–2).

Pacheco de Oliveira, J. (2019) *Exterminio y tutela: procesos de formación de alteridades en el Brasil*, Buenos Aires: UNSAM Edita.

Palavecino, E. (1928) Observaciones etnográficas sobre las tribus aborígenes del Chaco Occidental. *Anales de la Sociedad Argentina de Estudios Geográficos*, **3**, 188–214.

Palavecino, E. (1933) Los indios pilagás del Río Pilcomayo. *Anales del Museo Nacional de Historia Natural*, **37**, 317–382.

Prins, H. (2004) Visual Anthropology. In T. Biolsi (Ed.), *A Companion to the Anthropology of American Indians*. Oxford: Blackwell, pp. 506–525.

Ramos, A. (2011) Perspectivas antropológicas sobre la memoria en contextos de diversidad y desigualdad. *Alteridades* **21**, 131–148.

Rony, F. T. (1996) *The Third Eye. Race, Cinema and Ethnographic Spectacle*, Durham, NC: Duke University Press.

Russell, C. (2003) *Experimental Ethnography: The Work of Film in the Age of Video*. Durham, NC: Duke University Press.

Salomaa, I. (2002) *Rafael Karsten (1879–1956)* As a Finnish Scholar of Religion. The Life and Career of a Man of Science. Helsinki: Faculty of Arts, University of Helsinki.

Samuel, R. (1994) *Theatres of Memory: Past and Present in Popular Culture.* London & New York: Verso.

Sbardella, C., & Braunstein, J. (1991) Las dos caras de la tragedia de Fortín Yunka. *Hacia una nueva carta étnica del Gran Chaco,* **2,** 107–131.

Sbriccoli, T. (2016) Between the Archive and the Village: The Lives of Photographs in Time and Space. *Visual Studies,* **31,** 295–309.

Segato, R. (1998) The Color-Blind Subject of Myth; or Where to Find Africa in the Nation. *Annual Review of Anthropology,* **27,** 129–151.

Shohat, E., & Stam, R. (1994) *Unthinking Eurocentrism: Multiculturalism and the Media.* New York: Routledge.

Smith, L. (2006) *The Uses of Heritage.* London & New York: Routledge.

Smith, L. T. (1999) *Decolonizing Methodologies: Research and Indigenous Peoples.* London: Zed Books.

Spadafora, A., Gómez, M., & Matarrese, M. (2010) Rumbos y laberintos de la política étnica: organizaciones unificadas y faccionalismos índigenas en la provincia de Formosa (pilagá y toba). In G. Gordillo & S. Hirsch (Eds.), *Movilizaciones indígenas e identidades en disputa en la Argentina.* Buenos Aires: La Crujia, pp. 237–257.

Troya, M. (2012) Un segundo encuentro: la fotografía etnográfica dentro y fuera del archivo. *Íconos, Revista de Cienicas Sociales,* **42,** 17–31.

Vardich, Z. (2014) *Síntesis histórica de Las Lomitas y breves historias de su gente,* Formosa: Subsecretaria de la Cultura de la Provincia.

Veracini, L. (2010) *Settler Colonialism: A Theoretical Overview.* Houndmills, Palgrave Macmillan.

Vidal, A., & Telesca, I. (Eds.) (In Press) *Fortín Yunká (1919). Entre la Historia y Memoria del pueblo pilagá,* Buenos Aires: Sb.

Villarroel, M. (2010) Por la Ruta del Discurso Eurocéntrico en el Cine de Exploradores. *Aisthesis,* **48,** 90–111.

Vivaldi, A. (2016) Caminos a la ciudad, el monte y el Lote. Producción de lugares entre los Tobas (Qom) del Barrio Nam Qom, Formosa. *Corpus. Archivos virtuales de la alteridad americana,* **6**(1).

Vuoto, P. (1986) Los movimientos de Luciano y Pedro Martínez, dos cultos de transición entre los toba-taksek de Misión Tacaaglé. *Scripta Ethnológica,* **10,** 19–46.

Wassén, H. (Ed.) (1970) *Göteborgs Etnografiska Museum Årstryck 1969.* Gothenburg: Elanders boktryckeri aktiebolag.

Winter, T. (2013) Clarifying the Critical in Critical Heritage Studies. *International Journal of Heritage Studies*, **19**(6), 532–545.

Wright, C. (2009) Faletau's Photography or the Mutability of Visual History in Roviana. In E. Edwards & C. Morton (Eds.), *Photography, Anthropology and History: Expanding the Frame*. Farnhan & Burlington: Ashgate, pp. 223–240.

Wright, P. (2008) *Ser-en-el-sueño. Crónicas de historia y vida toba*, Buenos Aires: Biblos.

Cambridge Elements ≡

Critical Heritage Studies

Kristian Kristiansen
University of Gothenburg

Michael Rowlands
UCL

Francis Nyamnjoh
University of Cape Town

Astrid Swenson
Bath University

Shu-Li Wang
Academia Sinica

Ola Wetterberg
University of Gothenburg

About the Series

This series focuses on the recently established field of Critical Heritage Studies. Interdisciplinary in character, it brings together contributions from experts working in a range of fields, including cultural management, anthropology, archaeology, politics, and law. The series will include volumes that demonstrate the impact of contemporary theoretical discourses on heritage found throughout the world, raising awareness of the acute relevance of critically analysing and understanding the way heritage is used today to form new futures.

Cambridge Elements $\equiv$

Critical Heritage Studies

26507611R00046